This Gift Is Mine

This Gift Is Mine

Ralph W. Neighbour, Jr.

BROADMAN PRESS / Nashville, Tennessee

Grateful acknowledgment is made to the following for use of copyrighted material:

Oxford University Press for occasional quotations of texts from *The New English Bible.* Copyright © 1961, 1970 by The Delegates of the Oxford University Press and The Syndics of the Cambridge University Press.

Lois S. Hunsberger and *Faith at Work* for use of the poem appearing in *Faith at Work Magazine.* Reprinted by permission from *Faith at Work*, Columbia, Maryland 21044.

Dewey Decimal Classification Number: 248.4
Library of Congress Catalog Card Number: 73-93907
Printed in the United States of America

Lovingly,
I dedicate this book
as I have the others,
to the members of
West Memorial Baptist Church . . .
"The People Who Care."

Preface

As I typed the word above, my wife Ruth came into my office to tell me I had a long distance call. The time: 7 A.M., Saturday.

For the seven hundredth time since the story of *The People Who Care* was first released by the Associated Press in 1969, a heartbroken person in a distant city called for help. Sometimes it has been a couple with a shattered marriage 1,500 miles away. On other occasions it has been a parent asking us to help find a runaway.

I have marveled at the way God has used a little band of Christians, numbering near four hundred after five years, to meet needs of people all over the nation. As a result of the books *The Seven Last Words of the Church* and *The Touch of the Spirit,* scores of pastors have called or visited us.

I credit fellow members of this precious body with the writing of these pages. This book is the result of five years of dialogue with these men and women, and the sermons which have been the fruit of that constant exchange. The questions they have asked me about the gifts of the Spirit have caused the specifics to be discussed herein. I can assure the reader that this volume is distinctly a book of its age. I do not desire for it to be timeless: books are now published too rapidly for many of them to be worth reading twice!

To the *left* of the concept of the "spirituals" presented

in this volume is the highly charged charismatic movement, which continually nips at the heels of practically every body of believers in America. I have written this book so that a pastor with this problem can have something solid to place in the hands of the sheep. You may expect it to warn about wolves.

To the *right* of the concept of the "spirituals" presented in this volume is a highly uncharged traditionalism. It has annually filled vacant church offices with warm bodies, and totally ignored the teaching about the "spirituals" because they sounded too much like what was over on the left. I have written this book so that a pastor with this problem can have something solid to place in the hands of the sheep. You may expect it to warn about lethargy.

I have written it primarily for the laity, and have not tried to use technical theological terms. However, many of these pages have demanded three to five hours of research in the Greek.

But Fred didn't care about *how* my conclusions were reached. He didn't have time for all that. He's got a wife, kids, a good job, a fine church, and loves the Lord with all his heart. He didn't take his journey with me to argue about things. *He wanted information*! That level of trust is common among the laity in the Lord's body.

. . . And that's exactly why the wolves are having a heyday . . . and why I decided to go into the labor room and deliver another book, with all the pains which accompany it.

Frances Berner, your flying fingers have typed my books three times now! To you, I bequeath another thousand years removed from your stay in purgatory (I'm joking!). . . . To Pauline Lauterbach, a peck on the cheek for typing my sermons on the Gifts from our TOUCH Tape library. Thank you, dear Hester Powers, for proofreading until you had the blind staggers.

For you, dear reader, I bequeath an important passage from the Testament beside me which has pages falling all over the desk. It has been literally worn out studying about the gifts. I give you 1 Thessalonians 5:19-24: "Do not stifle inspiration, and do not despise prophetic utterances, but bring them all to the test and then keep what is good in them and avoid the bad of whatever kind.

"May God himself, the God of peace, make you holy *in every part*, and keep you sound in spirit, soul, and body, without fault when our Lord Jesus Christ comes. He who calls you is to be trusted; he will do it."

NOW, LET'S MEET FRED . . .

Contents

This Gift Is Mine

The pressure of duty—the demand
The doing because I ought
What of the gift?
Must it be hid because of someone's ought?
The gift is mine, and mine alone
So let me use it—not because I ought to
But—because I want to!
And using the gift I have
Let me call forth your gift,
So that together we may give the world
A gift so unique—so incredibly ours
That we may call other gifts into being.
And thus let the world see
Our gifts as Divine, God-given
Uniquely His—and used for Him.

Lois S. Hunsberger

1

Ordained, or Nominated?

Fred drove out of the church parking lot with frustration swelling up inside. For the *fourth time*, the nominating committee had ended a three-hour session with an incomplete roster of workers! With the annual business meeting only a week away, there would again be that last-minute committee meeting. For the third year in a row, he would spend *hours* on the phone, begging people to take church jobs for the coming year. Aloud, he muttered to himself, "And in a month, our committee will be back at work, plugging the holes left by people who *promised* us they would fill jobs, but never followed through."

He thought again of the Sunday School superintendent's statement in the meeting: "*This* year," he said, I don't want us to nominate Jane Dozem for Primary teacher! She's always thirty minutes late. And while I'm at it, I'd also appreciate our replacing this list of teachers. I'm sick and tired of their calling me at 9:00 o'clock on Sunday mornings, cancelling out because they 'have a cold' or 'their second cousin is visiting!' I have been run ragged all year trying to find last minute replacements."

Fred thought to himself, "*Something's wrong! Why should the Lord's work be run by those who are not really committed to what they are doing?*" He thought of his pastor. Why, that dear guy preached with a 100-degree fever last Sunday! Had to slip away from the service, drenched with sweat, to be driven home to bed by his wife. "If only *all* Christians could have the same sense of calling to their work that our pastor has," he mused. "Maybe we'll see a *real* revival meeting tear us loose some day . . . *then* it will be different."

FRED, THIS BOOK IS FOR YOU!

. . . And for all the others who, like you, cannot quite "buy" the problem of church members who respond reluctantly to a nominating committee's pleas "to serve." Fred, don't drive home just yet—turn right at the corner where Romans and 1 Corinthians merge at their twelfth chapters.

Got your seat belt fastened? . . .

. . . Then come along for a journey to the New Testament concept of spiritual gifts. We'll take a close look at what it was like "B.N.C." (Before Nominating Committees). We'll ride back to the days when the church was a *theocracy*: led by God directly—rather than a *democracy*: led by men trying to do God's work on his behalf. If the road back seems bumpy, don't be alarmed. It's safe enough. It has an eroded surface because it has been a long time since the Lord's children have traveled it.

Oh . . . and by the way: that bubbly-looking side road running parallel to us is filled with *quicksand*. Don't drive over there! Some time ago I heard someone call that road by the name, "Abuses." Those who try to get to the gifts by using that road always sink into the quagmire of "experiences." The road we are going to use has a lovely name. It was paved by Paul, and he named it . . .

"THE MORE EXCELLENT WAY."

See? It is printed on that signpost over there. Straight on, Fred. No curves in sight. . . . But watch out for that pothole! Let's hope that by the time we get ready to return, others will have come after us, and will care enough about this road to have it freshly paved.

2
The Giver of the Gift

" 'Repent,' said Peter, 'repent and be baptized, every one of you, in the name of Jesus the Messiah for the forgiveness of your sins; and you will receive *the gift of the Holy Spirit*" (Acts 2:38).

Fred, I know you must be exposed to many new doctrinal teachings. Some of your friends have become confused about the relationship between the Christian and the Holy Spirit? I'm not surprised! Well, as we drive along together, it might be important for us to discuss that. Let's begin with some basics:

We all started on an equal footing before God—rebellious! Not a one among us reached out to God as children, seeking to know him in his fullness. One by one, we each decided to become the gods of our own existences. In our separate ways, we told God to mind his own business, and we'd mind ours.

Then the Holy Spirit came to communicate with us. He began to dog our path, and we became aware of our sin, the coming judgment, and God's righteousness.

Here's an important point! Our relationship to the Holy Spirit started *before we became Christians*. We didn't have to seek *him—he* sought *us*.

His deliberate intention back in the days of our rejection was to point us toward Jesus Christ. The God who is

Spirit, who chose to reveal himself, did so by placing his life within the body of Mary's baby. So significant was this act that her pregnancy was *caused* by the Holy Spirit. Jesus Christ is God's ultimate way of revealing himself.

The Holy Spirit was sent into our lives to draw us to Jesus Christ. The Spirit opens our prejudiced eyes to see that Christ's death on the cross is a very *personal* act. He died for *each one of us*. Not only was the nature of *God* in that body on the cross: *our sin was also there*. He died for our sin, bearing its load. In doing so, he provided the only available connection between the Father and mankind.

Fred, the point I am making is that the work of the Holy Spirit has begun before we become Christians. He first came to point us to Christ.

When we became Christians, we did so by receiving a new relationship with Christ. Christ literally came to take up residence in our lives when we met God's terms.

Those terms have been set forth clearly in Romans 10. They require us to have *more* than just a *knowledge* of our sin and Christ's substitutionary death. The terms also require far more than just *believing* that the knowledge we have received is true. *God's terms require us to confess we want Jesus Christ to be the Lord of our lives.*

"Lord" is a powerful word in the Greek language. It involves our giving up all personal privilege, all self-control. Literally, it means: "He to whom a person belongs, about which he has the power of deciding."

The act of becoming a Christian is a commitment in which I give *me up*, lock, stock, and barrel, to Jesus Christ. It is an unconditional surrender! There is no compromise or alternative.

God's terms are clear-cut: "If you want to be a member of my family, you must receive my Son into your life, asking him unconditionally to be your sovereign Owner!"

At this point, Jesus Christ takes up residence inside the life. He does more than "walk with me, and talk with me;" Ephesians 5:30 says literally, "for members we are of his body, of his flesh, and of his bones." A man is never the same again when he discovers Christ dwelling *inside* his life!

14

Galatians 3:26-28 describes the new relationship in awesome thoughts: "For through faith you are all sons of God in union with Christ Jesus. Baptized into union with him, you have all put on Christ as a garment. There is no such thing as Jew and Greek, slave and freeman, male and female; for you are all one person in Christ Jesus."

His entrance into our life is marked by a wonderful gift he gives to us. The moment we receive Christ as Lord, God sets us apart for himself and makes us his holy temple. At that moment, we are given THE GIFT—*the Holy Spirit*.

Peter explained in Acts 2:38 that at the time of repentance we would receive not just *gifts*, but *the gift* of the Holy Spirit. In Acts 10:45 the *gift* of the Holy Spirit is again described as entering the Gentiles as they were converted. He comes as a *gift* at the beginning of our salvation.

Actually, Fred, the Bible never teaches that we are baptized, or immersed, *into* the Holy Spirit! What *is* taught is quite different. The Holy Spirit comes to us before we are Christians, convicting us. Then, at the time of our confession, *the Holy Spirit baptizes us into union with Christ.* When Christ enters us to establish residence, our baptism *by* the Holy Spirit has taken place. No other baptism is ever taught in the New Testament. There is "one Lord, one faith, one baptism"!

Colossians 2:12 affirms this: "For in baptism you were buried with him [Christ], in baptism also you were raised to life with him through your faith in the active power of God who raised him from the dead."

To be baptized into Jesus Christ by the Holy Spirit marks the beginning of the Christian life. *It also marks the entrance of the Holy Spirit, God's indwelling Gift.* As he came to me *before* conversion to point me to Jesus Christ, so he remains *after* conversion *for the same purpose*: "When he comes who is the Spirit of truth, he will guide you into all the truth; for he will not speak on his own authority, but will tell only what he hears; and . . . he will glorify me, for everything that he makes known to you he will draw from what is mine" (John 16:13-14).

Jesus is the giver, and the Holy Spirit who indwells us is

the gift we receive.

John tells us, "Here is the proof that we dwell in him and he dwells in us: He has imparted his Spirit to us." (1 John 4:13). The fact that I know the Holy Spirit dwells in me is my assurance that I am a Christian!

But Fred, all I have said so far has been necessary to lead up to the big point I want to make—*by the Holy Spirit, I am baptized into the body of Christ*. First Corinthians 12:12 says, "For Christ is like a single body with its many limbs and organs, which, many as they are, together make up one body."

Here we are introduced to a mystical union. Jesus Christ is the "head" of a "body": that is, he is Lord over the church in the same sense that a brain controls the activity of a human body. To be united to him is to be a part of what he controls. At the moment the Holy Spirit joins us to him, he also joins us to all the other parts of his body—all who have also responded to his lordship.

It's really not *my place* to join myself to the body. That is the work of the Holy Spirit. This is a pretty fantastic thought, Fred! Think through with me some of the ramifications of it:

1. The true body of Christ is made up of others who, like myself, have truly confessed Jesus Christ as Lord. Membership rolls kept by church clerks don't tell the real truth. The *true* membership of the body is limited to the ones who are committed to his lordship. When your nominating committee meets, does it recognize the fact that the wheat and the tares are growing up together? It's about as impossible to get "Christian service" out of an unregenerate church member as it would be to persuade a corpse to perform on a stage.

2. The *true* body, called the "church," is comprised *only* of those who are baptized into it by the work of the Holy Spirit. In today's culture we are a long way from understanding the meaning of 1 Corinthians 12:18: "God appointed each limb and organ to its own place in the body, as he chose."

How does the average Christian select the church he will join? He may possibly weigh such matters as: quality of

preaching, newness of buildings, adequacy of choir, effective-
ness of youth program, size of congregation, proximity to
home . . . *ad nauseam*! A dentist I know chose *not* to join a
small, new congregation nearby because he said, "It would
not be large enough to bring me as many patients as the
3,000 member church down the freeway." (Try to nominate
him to a position of sacrificial service, Fred!)

What kind of a *freak* does a church become when it sets
no biblical standard for membership? That standard is clear:
the test for church membership should be . . .

a. Are you one who has acknowledged the lordship of
Christ?

b. Has the Holy Spirit appointed you to a place in this
body? Are you aware of *his* appointment to this church?

It's mighty hard for the Head to direct the functions of
the limbs when there is no clear connection between them to
begin with! This is the curse of the church today—and it will
remain as the status quo until the biblical standard is *required*
for membership.

Back in my college days I worked in a speech correction
clinic. Mary Jane had an hourly meeting with me each day.
She was a spastic. Her grades were straight "A"s in every college course. Nothing wrong with her mind! But I used to hurt
as I watched her leave our sessions together. She would be
limp and exhausted from the strain of trying to make her
frail body respond to her desire to speak whole sentences.
Her lungs would decide to inhale in the middle of a word.
Her neck would twist her head sideways in the middle of a
sentence. How I admired her as I saw her strong mind try to
bring rebellious muscles under control! *Similar to dear Mary
Jane is the church comprised of those who are not jointly
committed to the Head, who desire to "do their own thing."*

The Holy Spirit baptized us into Christ, and he also
baptized us into his body. In that transaction, Christ, the
Head of the body, presented the gift of the Holy Spirit to
the members as the connection between him and them. The
Spirit was made the spokesman from the Head to the limbs.
The Spirit can be confident that the limbs will obey the Head,
for he himself placed each limb in its power position!

Fred, we're just about to arrive at our destination. As we study the function of the gifts, we must remember the relationship which started when we were baptized into Christ. If we do, we'll not be so surprised at the way this early New Testament church functioned as a *theocracy*, not a *democracy*.

3
The Meaning of "Gifts"

"About gifts of the Spirit, there are some things of which I do not wish you to remain ignorant. . . . In each of us the Spirit is manifested in one particular way, for some useful purpose" (1 Cor. 12:1-7).

When the Head of the body enters our life, we are placed into that body quite deliberately! We are given a *practical* function to perform. A hand or an eye must do its specific job in the body's life. The human body is an amazing creation —everything does *something*!

Fred, when I was a little boy in about the third grade, my teacher told me that the reason we could wiggle our ears was because during the process of evolutionary development we were a lower form of animal life. Back in those days, he explained, our ears flopped over like a dog's ears. It seemed that we needed muscles in our ears to lift them up so we could hear better. Later, as man developed into his higher stages, the muscles remained in the ear as a remnant of that lesser stage. My teacher assured us that the muscle had no earthly use now!

Believing that Genesis gives us more intelligent information about man's beginning than my schoolteacher, I decided to ask my visiting great uncle, a physician, about the matter. (He knew everything!) Uncle Ernest explained to me that my teacher was full of prunes. The involuntary twitching of the muscle was the only way old blood could be removed and fresh blood inserted into the cartilage area of the ear. Were that muscle to be severed, he explained, the ear would turn black!

God was up to something when he put muscles in our ears. And when the Holy Spirit baptized us into the body of Jesus Christ, he was up to something, too!

First Corinthians 12:7 explains what he's up to: personally, carefully, the Spirit is given to our lives so we might function "for some useful purpose." Therefore, the Christ-given *Gift* comes to us with *gifts*.

In 1 Corinthians 12:1, the term "gifts of the Spirit" is, in the Greek, simply "*the spirituals*." That term describes specific capacities produced in us by the entrance of the Holy Spirit. It means that I have received spiritual abilities, so that I might perform adequately as a member of Christ's body.

The Spirit's life within me is a *practical* possession. He is not mine to enjoy having, as I would enjoy playing with a toy. He has indwelled me to use me to perform the tasks directed by the Head.

My new "spirituals" make it possible for me to function. Let's compare this to a hand. When God shapes a human body in the loins of a woman, he arranges the bone, muscle, nerve, flesh, blood vessels, and skin of the hand in a certain fashion. Hold your hand in front of you: each finger is a different length. This makes it possible for them to function individually against the thumb. Now, fold your fingers into the palm: they are now all the same length! When they go to work in unison to pick up a shovel handle, they are uniquely designed for their new task. We could go on, thinking about the placement of the nerve endings, etc. The hand was carefully designed to do its task.

The God who outfitted the human body has also outfitted the body of Christ. Paul says, "For just as in a single human body there are many limbs and organs, all with different functions, so all of us, united with Christ, form one body, serving individually as limbs and organs to one another" (Rom. 12:4-5).

Then he goes on to say (. 6): "The gifts we possess differ as they are allotted to us by God's grace, and must be exercised accordingly." Here, he uses a different Greek word for *gifts*. This time the word is not "spirituals," but a word meaning "grace gifts." This second word is frequently used in the New Testament to describe our new spiritual capacities. The significance of it is that it ties the idea of our gifts to the *grace of God*.

As all Sunday School scholars know, "grace" means "unmerited favor"—God has given me something I did not deserve. He did not present me with my gifts because I was highly skilled, or properly born, or spiritually perfect. God felt no obligation to me! My place in the Lord's body is an act of *grace*. My function as a member of that body is an act of *grace*. My service for him, using the "spirituals," is a function of *grace*.

There isn't a single reason why I should ever brag about my gifts! Nor is there any earthly reason why I should be jealous over the "spirituals" possessed by another member of the body. He has them by grace.

When I was born into the physical world, I was endowed with certain talents related to my function in it. The use of these human talents, or skills, makes it possible for me to contribute to human society. Man's ability to paint, to be an accountant, or to design a bridge, makes him a productive person.

Paul tells us that when we are united to Christ, "There is a new world." What is that new "world"? Jesus described it for Nicodemus (John 3) as the "kingdom of God." He told Nicodemus that until he had been born over again, he would not so much as even possess the faculty of eyes to *see* that new world! The kingdom of God is entered by the new birth. When one is born again, he is baptized into Christ's body—and receives certain faculties necessary to function adequately in the new environment.

The "spirituals" are given to us in order that we might be productive, functioning members of that new world. THEY ARE OBVIOUSLY MUCH MORE THAN OUR NATURAL, OR PHYSICAL, TALENTS!

The unbeliever does not possess the "spirituals," because *he does not possess the Spirit*. The coming of the Spirit marks the coming of the "spirituals."

We have missed the teaching of the Scripture if we think that "spiritual gifts" refers to using natural talents for the glory of God. A man playing the piano in church instead of a beer joint is not exercising his spiritual "gift." He is simply using his natural talents for the glory of God, rather than for the devil.

There is a whole *"world"* of difference between the *talent* of teaching practiced by the atheistic college professor, and the *gift* of teaching practiced by the Bible expositor! And because a person can sing beautifully before the sermon does not necessarily mean the person is using a "spiritual."

Let me illustrate: Some years ago I shared a week of evangelistic meetings with a talented soloist. She had a national reputation, and drew crowds nightly. Just before I stood to preach, she would spellbind the people with her delivery. I began to shrink from facing the audience after she finished: they were breathless! I found it impossible to begin to preach. The congregation was not prepared to "consider Jesus"; they had to be "talked down" before the sermon could be introduced.

This woman had a fantastic *talent*, but she was not manifesting "spirituals" by her platform work. I was relieved when the meeting closed.

Perhaps three years passed. Then I noticed that she was scheduled to sing just before I spoke to a state evangelism conference in the Southeast. My plane arrived an hour late, and I was rushed to the municipal auditorium minutes before my scheduled message. I did not have time to visit with the soloist before she stood to sing, and I anticipated the worst.

My soul! I have never before experienced what occurred in those eight minutes she sang before the audience! When she finished, we were all left at the foot of Mount Calvary, adoring our blessed Savior. Quietly, unnoticed, that godly woman slipped to her chair.

The only sensible thing to do was to lead the audience in a season of worship and adoration. I never used my prepared message. The Holy Spirit took control, and he flowed like a river of living water into our midst.

When the service was concluded, I drew her into the stage wings and said, "What has happened to you since we last met?" With joy, she replied, "Oh! Ralph! Does it *show*?" Softly I answered, "Yes, it shows. Your risen Lord showed himself to us all!"

During lunch, she shared with us how the Spirit had done a deep work within her life. For years she had proudly displayed her "talent," never caring about the deep things of God. Then she began to see herself for what she was—a Christian worker totally bankrupt within. She shared how agonizing it had been to abandon the old ways, and what peace had flooded her heart as she abandoned herself to the lordship of Christ. No longer confused about the source of her capacities, the life of the Spirit had been released within her.

The "spirituals" of the functioning member of the body had blessed us with all spiritual blessings—and the Spirit within her had transported us to heavenly places. *Furthermore, it didn't happen only when she was singing on a platform!* Her "spirituals" had a way of propelling people past her to Jesus—on the elevator, in the prayer meeting, flying in the airplane, *just everywhere*! Her function in the kingdom of God was to be a signpost, pointing men to the Head.

I guess we'd have to call her a "finger" in the body! Specifically, an *index* finger. Right hand. Pointing up.

If she sings in your town, you'll find out what I mean. Her name is . . . Joe Ann Shelton!

Fred, my heart aches when I think of the thousands of dear Christians who have not understood that practicing their earthly *talents* in church work is totally foreign to exercising grace-given "spirituals." Indeed, because they *are* using their talents, many are blind to the very fact that they even *possess* grace-gifts.

True, sometimes the talents and the gifts may coincide—but not necessarily. I am thinking of one godly pastor who had the spiritual gift of preaching, but stuttered terribly in all other speaking situations. To the day of his retirement, he never got victory over that disorder, but it never stopped him from exercising his holy *gift*. I have heard others *speak* from pulpits, whose delivery was silky smooth, and whose voices were resonant, and who never *preached* at all. There is a great contrast between after-dinner speakers and preachers—and it is infinitely more than tables *vs.* pews! It's talent *vs.* gift.

Another thing about this subject—great difficulty occurs when the hand tries to function as a wrist or an elbow! Long before I knew anything about living inside the "spirituals" in my ministry, I used to think that the gifts of preaching, teaching, and evangelism were all synonymous. The pastor in the adjoining county would invite me to leave my pastorate and come to a "week of evangelistic meetings." I would accept. (The fact that my family needed the honorarium *desperately* had nothing to do with it!)

There, I would be introduced as *"Evangelist* Ralph Neighbour." That sounded pretty good! Kind of put me in the same league with Billy Graham . . .

The trouble was, I was always miserable in my spirit during these weeks. I would put that nagging feeling behind me, however, and keep on plodding. As the years passed, the size of the "campaigns" kept increasing. After a few "city-wide" meetings, the old ego said, "You know, you ought to do this full time!"

It was about that time the Holy Spirit first began to teach me the truths about the "spirituals." It all came home to roost in a West Texas town about six years ago, during a county-wide crusade. I spent the most miserable week of my life there, with my picture plastered all over town. The meeting was "successful," insofar as God honored his Word and scores of folks were converted, but I have never been more conscious that I was totally out of my place in the body! What a relief it was to finally look in the mirror and say to my reflection, "Mister, you are NOT given the necessary combination of 'spirituals' required for this ministry!"

I can only remember one time when I was any more miserable. It was when I was a college student, and I got a fat-paying job working on a roofing gang. Now, a scholar of books I may be—but a burner of tar I am not. I nearly *kissed* the grimy foreman who fired me! What a joy it was to be able to say to myself, "You are not now—nor shall you ever be—a candidate for a roofing gang."

It causes me no pangs of guilt at all these days to kindly thank the pastors who invite me to come and be an "evangelist," and refer them instead to a couple of members of the body I know well who have the gifts required to do this kind of preaching. (As we shall see later, there is a distinction to be made between evangelistic *preaching* and the work of the *office of an evangelist*.)

Now, recognizing my own spiritual gifts, I joyfully accept those invitations which fit them: teaching, exhorting, prophesying, leading, giving, helping others in distress, distinguishing true spirits from false. My only regret is that someone did not sit me down during school days and spell all these things out. You live and learn!

Fred, I know the uppermost question in your mind just now is, "How do you discover your gifts?" Obviously, we'll get around to answering that for you—but there are some things we need to clear up first.

4

Legs Belong to Bodies

"A body is not one single organ, but many . . . The eye cannot say to the hand, 'I do not need you' " (1 Cor. 12:14-21).

Nothing is more foreign to the New Testament than the idea that spiritual gifts are to be exercised privately, or that the individual receives them for personal enrichment.

Fred, you and I are not "Lone Ranger" Christians. A believer is missing what God made him to be when he is not intimately joined to a local body of Christians, called the "church."

Salvation of the individual is a *personal* thing, but the very act joins us to the church, the "family of God." For one to be a member of the family demands an active relationship with its members at all times.

John warns against hating other members of the family. Paul tells us that members of the family are never to be un-equally yoked to nonfamily members. Hebrews cautions us against neglecting fellowship with our brothers and sisters. Peter describes the family as a group of "living stones," care-fully fitted to each other. We belong to each other.

When we study the Scriptures about the gifts of the Spirit, other descriptions of the church seem weak in contrast. So powerful is the analogy drawn in 1 Corinthians 12 that nothing could ever be written to exceed it! *The intimacy of the family is described in terms of the union of parts of a human body.* Paul says, "I'm a hand; you're a foot. There's a liver, and I also see a lung. We Christians cannot exist without each other."

Then . . . the powerful words of verses 27-28: "Now you are Christ's body, and each of you a limb or organ of it. Within our community God has appointed . . . apostles . . . prophets . . . teachers . . ." As we grasp his teaching, we realize that each gift is given in order that it will be profitable to the body.

Each spiritual gift presented to the body is within the life of a Christian. Each new Christian added to a body will provide a needed gift for it to function.

When God wants the body to be teaching, he will provide by his sovereign act a person with the gift of teaching. No teacher has a right to "hang out a shingle" and teach apart from the body! His gift belongs to the congregation.

A member of the body who does not *possess* the gift of teaching should never be asked to do so! The number of teachers God has added to a local congregation will always be the exact number necessary for the body to function.

The church gets into trouble when it decides in a committee meeting that it needs "X" number of classes, and then tries to find enough warm bodies to fill the teachers' chairs. It would be much better to have one large group, taught by a God-gifted teacher, than ten groups, nine of which are being bored by "feet" trying to function as "hands"!

God's order is the reverse of man's order. Man first decides how many *classes* will be taught. God first decides how many *teachers* the body needs. The difference between a *gifted* teacher and a *non*gifted teacher is not determined by the ability to prepare a lesson adequately and deliver it smoothly. Rather, it is revealed by the presence of God communicated through the teacher!

Poor Fred! Your nominating committee has not yet given thought to the matter of how many feet, ears, hands, and eyes the body possesses. Your concern has been the number of steps to be walked, words to be heard, tasks to be done, pictures to be seen, by the body's annual calendar of activities. How much *simpler* it would be to realize that the body's ministry at any given moment need be no greater than the functioning members.

Some members of the body may latently be teachers, but may require another three years of growing, from "young men" to "fathers" (1 John 2:13), before the Holy Spirit will call them to service. It is a deadly thing to nominate them before the Spirit calls them!

During ten years of preaching in different churches nearly every week, I made it a practice to arrive early enough to attend Sunday School classes. I would always say to the superintendent, "Put me in the adult class with the most *gifted* teacher." In well over 70 percent of those classes, the teachers were lacking in the most elementary levels of spiritual insight. In far more classes than I care to admit, lessons were read *verbatim* from a quarterly, or the last pro football game was requarterbacked for half the teaching period.

Would it not have been wiser to let the *pastor*, if no one else, teach those adults? Should the kingdom suffer violence of this sort? Is it ever logical to expect a thumb to hear, or a toe to smell? Should it not be the first order of business for a local body to discern, member by member, the assets of spiritual gifts available for ministry? Does it not sound reasonable to emphasize the discovery of those gifts by each member, rather than the filling of jobs by a committee? Can the Holy Spirit be trusted to call the members of the body to their ministries?

A few years ago Robert Girard rattled my cage with his book, *Brethren, Hang Loose*. In it he described a drastic decision made by his congregation: "Anything in the church program that cannot be maintained without constant pastoral pressure on people to be involved should be allowed to die a sure and natural death."

That fit a biblical pattern! If God wants a body to walk, he'll give it a pair of legs. To force a torso to walk is agony for both the forcer and the torso.

I had to admit I was a forcer of torsos! For example, that plagued bus ministry I started had never gotten off the ground, in spite of endless hours spent encouraging members to "get to work."

Somewhere about that same time the Lord taught me another lesson: He wasn't interested in *what* we did . . . only in whether *he started it*! I winced as I admitted to myself that I had started the bus ministry. Not one gifted member had been called to that work.

Oh, wretched ego trip! The Yellow Monster on wheels stared at me from its spot on the gaoline station parking lot every time I drove by, saying, "Ralph, YOU started me . . . and I won't run!"

Finally, I decided to recommend Bob Girard's rule, in the form of a motion to the church in our monthly business meeting. With almost a hilarious shout, the body passed the motion unanimously. The Yellow Monster sold in four days for six hundred dollars. Other pastor-pushed programs died without so much as a murmur.

Oh, the butterflies that followed in the stomach of the body's undershepherd! Could I *really* trust the Giver of Gifts to call his ministers into service? As classes became vacant, Harold (my associate) and I began to pray for gifted members to be *called* to the teaching needs.

Gradually it started to work! The story is told on pages 62-71 of my book *The Seven Last Words of the Church* (Zondervan, 1973). TOUCH ministries started spontaneously during the days following, teachers came forth to teach, and the two "coaches" (pastors) found themselves working feverishly as equippers rather than forcers.

West Memorial has now functioned under this new policy for several years. At this writing, we have more teachers than we have classes to be taught! The logical result of our new policy has caused us to start new classes for Bible study, both on Sunday and during the week, as the body gifts are discovered. Our current growth is taking place on this simple premise:

1. This body has a Head. He is Jesus Christ.

2. The body is made up exclusively of members put into it by the Holy Spirit.

3. Each member brings spiritual gifts. They are to be exercised for the glory of the Head, and for the witness and ministry of the body.

4. The undershepherds are called to help the members find and develop the use of their gifts.

5. God, according to his timetable, can be trusted to call forth our *ministries* through the gifted members.

6. These ministries will comprise the sum total of the activity of the body.

7. *All* members of the body are ministers. They are called to their ministry in the exact same way that a preacher is called to preach: first, the gift; then, the Spirit's call; finally, *obedience*.

A significant truth began to emerge for us. We realized that some ministries existed only because a gift had been placed within the body. What would happen to that ministry when the gifted member moved to another state? Should we harp at the toes to do the job of the thumb? Of course not! If the ministry should be continued, God would raise up a new thumb.

At the time of writing these words, we have just seen another instance of God's Spirit directing us in this matter. Some months ago, one of our gals began a TOUCH ministry called "HOPE." (That stands for "Helping Others Practice English.) It grew and grew. Our Ann thrived on this ministry. At one point, she tried to add a weekday Bible study as a second ministry, but somehow it never survived. Eventually, Ann told me that she was learning more about her gifts, and they rested in the HOPE ministry. She settled down to a meaningful place of service. Many women from Buddhist countries were being reached for Christ through this every-Tuesday evangelism.

Imagine the bombshell when Gerald was transferred to faraway New Jersey! My initial reaction to him when he stopped by my house to tell me was to say, "Gerald, it's going to be expensive to commute from Houston to New

Jersey every day!" *What would happen to HOPE?*

Delightedly, we knew that *God* had started HOPE, and *he* had a problem! Committing it to him to solve, we accepted the fact that if he felt the ministry should be continued, he would call forth the proper leader with spiritual gifts. Instead of calling for a meeting of the nominating committee, I wrote to the body, saying: "MINISTER, WHERE ARE YOU?"

One of the sweetest gals in our body had, in the meantime, been growing in her faith walk. Not in the "nick" of time, but in *God's* time, she was spiritually ready to step into the vacancy to be left by Ann. HOPE just now is still growing like a weed!

Then, Bill and Betty came to see me. Parents of a retarded child, they had organized from scratch our FLOC ministry, which consists of a Thursday night sharing group for parents of exceptional children. (God started *that* ministry, too, without any help from the "Holy Man"!) Bill's transfer to a distant city meant the FLOC ministry was in jeopardy. Instantly, the three of us agreed that whether FLOC lived or died would be the Lord's place to decide. Perhaps it was too closely related to two people of the body to be carried on by anyone else.

At this moment, I still don't know what the Spirit will do with that ministry. One fine couple is praying just now about what may be God's call to take it over. They have grown immensely since coming to Christ, and are potentially gifted in areas which might make their calling to FLOC a reality.

Pastor Ralph is relaxed about the matter. My hard work does not begin with talking someone into taking over a job. It awaits the appointment of the Spirit. If this new couple are *called* to shepherd FLOC, then as the spiritual coach I will be involved in the equipping ministry. I love that work!

We have noticed a radical change in the conduct of the ministers toward their ministry since we began operating under these biblical principles. The body recognizes that we are each one called to minister. Since our ministries were not started at the church office, that's not the place to go to dump your problems! Teachers who are *called* to teach will let their visiting second cousins choose between coming along to church—or sitting in an empty house until noon on Sunday!

Each one of us realizes that if we flop in our ministry, "it will die a sure and natural death!" We don't *have* to have a certain ministry functioning. The church *can* exist solely on the basis of what God has called the members of the body to do!

"Whatever gift each of you may have received, use it in service to one another, like good stewards dispensing the grace of God in its varied forms" (1 Peter. 4:10).

5

"You Get Bornded That Way!"

"Everyone has the gift God has granted him, one this gift and another that" (1 Cor. 7:7).

While visiting one day, a mother left me alone with her little four-year old. Wondering if Jonathan knew the Old Testament history of his name, I said: "Son, do you know why you were named 'Jonathan?' "

He gave me a "I-think-all-adults-are-stupid" look, and marched out of the room with the comment, "Sure. I got *bornded* that way!"

Spiritual gifts are given as Jonathan's name was given. His parents decided before he was *"bornded"* what they wanted him to be called. He was not given the right to approach them at age six or sixteen and say, "Folks, I'd like to be named Jeremiah." It was the sovereign right of his parents to choose his name.

Fred, in the same way, it is the privilege of God to bestow his gifts upon his children. He decides, without any advice from the children, *what* gifts shall be given to *each* of them. His choices are made upon the basis of what he intends for us to reveal about him through our lives. Each of us has been equipped to share something unique about his indwelling life. For a fuller discussion of this, see pages 37-53 of my book *The Touch of the Spirit* (Broadman, 1972). He knew prior to establishing the world's foundations which ones of us could best minister in his name through teaching, or by administration, or by helping others.

The *ways* of God are clearly taught by Scriptures dealing with this subject. For example, 1 Corinthians 12:18 says: "God *appointed* each limb and organ to its own place in the body, *as he chose*." The context indicates that "limbs" and "organs" refer to Christians with specific spiritual gifts.

Romans 12:6 teaches the identical truth: "The gifts we possess differ *as they are allotted to us* by God's grace, and must be exercised accordingly." Clearly, he does the deciding, and we do the receiving. Which gift we receive is something about which we can make no choice.

Hebrews 2:4 states: "God added his testimony . . . by distributing the gifts of the Holy Spirit *at his own will*." We're staring squarely at the sovereignty of God in connection with the receiving of spiritual gifts!

First Corinthians 12:24 affirms the same doctrine with this explanation: "God has combined the various parts of the body . . . so that there might be no sense of division in the body." Get the message? There is to be no holier-than-thou attitude among Christians who say, "If you were as spiritual as I, you'd possess the gift God has given me!"

Billy Graham has frequently pointed out that his own ministry, internationally known, is no more significant before God than that of a simple housewife who ministers for her Lord day-by-day within the confines of a small home. His wife, Ruth, has placed above her kitchen sink a plaque reading: "Divine Service Is Rendered Here Daily." Ruth does not aspire in her prayer life to be an evangelist: her own spiritual gifts, sovereignly bestowed and divinely used, are in a totally different area!

We have no right to ask God to give us any spiritual gift. To do so is to infringe upon his sovereignty.

In commenting upon 1 Corinthians 12:14-21, my dear friend Ron Dunn has commented: "Just suppose that ten toes got together some night and decided to pray that they would all be given the gift of seeing. Or, suppose an eye from the head came to them saying, "Toes, you really haven't got it *all* yet! You need to ask God to give you the gift of seeing." Suppose the toes all pray, and pray, and pray . . . until God finally agrees to give them the gift of seeing. *What would they see? . . . The inside of a sock!"*

One of the absurdities of this generation is the idea that we can receive gifts by *asking* for them. The bestowal of spiritual gifts was determined by God before we were ever born—physically or spiritually!

In Romans 9, Paul discusses God's words to Rebekah in regard to the twins in her womb. In verses 11 and 12 he says, "In order that God's selective purpose might stand, *based not upon men's deeds* but upon the call of God, she was told, even before they were born, when they had as yet done nothing, good or ill, 'the elder shall be servant to the younger.' "

The *ways* of God! He knew (Eph. 1:3-10) "before the world was founded" which ones of us were to become his children, and his holy purpose for each of us was settled just that long ago. He does not bless Christians with spiritual gifts as a reward for their deeds. Before we did anything, good or bad, that matter was settled.

Further, gifts are not a reward for being filled with the Spirit. The result of the Spirit-filled life is not the receiving of a gift: *it is the bearing of fruit . . . the fruit of the Spirit.* Galatians 5 lists the fruit: "love, joy, peace, patience, kindness, goodness, fidelity, gentleness, and self-control."

To any casual observer, it is obvious that some Christians exercise their spiritual gifts without revealing the precious fruit mentioned. I'm thinking of a man who is one of the greatest Bible teachers I have ever known . . . gifted beyond question . . . who on occasion has made me want to hide under the table because of his rudeness to restaurant waitresses. No fruit!

That's what 1 Corinthians 13 is all about: "I may have the *gift* . . . but if I have no *love* [fruit!] I am nothing" (v. 2). How the heart of God must ache when untaught Christians gather to ask him for gifts, when he taught us instead to

35

seek after the life of total obedience which alone will produce fruit.

When are the gifts received? At the moment of my new birth! "Flesh can give birth only to flesh; it is spirit that gives birth to spirit" (John 3:6). At the moment I am born over again—as I am placed in Jesus Christ's holy life—as the Holy Spirit occupies my life as his temple—at this moment, which we refer to as the instant of conversion, I receive all the spiritual gifts I shall ever possess. It is at the time of salvation that I am, once and forever, "brought into one body by baptism, in the one Spirit" (1 Cor. 12:13). The Spirit of God is his greatest gift to me at the time of my conversion. To understand 1 Corinthians 12, we must understand that the coming of the Holy Spirit involves his joining me to the body of Christ. In order for me to be joined to the body, I must be placed within it as a hand, a foot, an inward part, etc. To be so placed requires me to have, *at the instant of my conversion,* my spiritual gifts!

The entrance of the Holy Spirit at conversion brings with it the gifts. Simply and only because he has come, I have received my gifts. They are *"based not upon men's deeds!"*

Even as John 3 parallels the physical and spiritual births, so we can parallel physical and spiritual gifts. When a baby is born, he has latent within his tiny frame, skills to be developed by exercise, education, etc., but we will never add to them. His basic intelligence, his final height, manual dexterity (or lack of it), are given at birth. He has a latent power to reproduce sexually—but he will have to wait some dozen years or so for it to become operative. In a matter of *minutes,* however, he will exercise the ability to suck milk with his facial muscles.

Still later, the little baby will begin to develop mentally, but certain latent skills of logic await the maturity of adulthood. The point to be made just now is, *nothing is added later on!* He does not return to his mother after he learns to walk, saying, "Mom, now please give me my arms and hands." Nor does he ask her later to reward him with ears because he has learned to see.

When God places his holy life in us, we are born again. When we are born again, we are placed in the body. When we are placed in the body, we are *gifted* with spiritual skills needed for us to function adequately as a part of the body.

"Can the pot speak to the potter and say, 'Why did you make me like this?'? Surely the potter can do what he likes with the clay" (Rom. 9:20-21). Mine is not the task of *getting* gifts: it is the task of *discovering* them. It is also the task of the Holy Spirit to use the ingredient of time to mature—to shape, to "sandpaper"—my spiritual life, so certain latent gifts can be brought forth for use. Until *he* knows I am mature enough to exercise them, they will not be made available—*no matter how much I beg for them!* The Holy Spirit would no more permit them to be used than a mother would give a three month old baby a pair of sharp scissors.

This is the very fabric from which 1 Corinthians 14:1 is cut.

The Greek says literally, "be most eagerly desirous of spiritual gifts." Believers have been *latently endowed*. Spiritual maturity will be needed to reveal some gifts, and obedience and faith will be required for discovering all. No one will be "zapped" with a gift simply because he wants something he does not possess.

"But each of us *has been given* [note the past tense?] his gift, his due portion of Christ's bounty. Therefore Scripture says: . . . 'He gave gifts to men' " (Eph. 4:7-8).

"You get *bornded* that way!"

6
Coins in the Fountain

"The water that I shall give him will be an inner spring always welling up for eternal life" (John 4:14). "There are varieties of gifts, but the same Spirit" (1 Cor. 12:4).

At the intersection of Romans 12 and 1 Corinthians 12, there is a lovely well. Called the "Holy Spirit," this clear source of divine water is the great gift the Head has given to the body parts. Fred, if you'll lean over just a little more as you look, you'll see some shining objects within the "inner spring." They are the *"spirituals."*

As this holy well is implanted in each of us, one or more of those "spirituals" will be found within it. Let's consider them as *coins in the fountain!*

Count closely, and you'll discover there are eleven of those coins. If you note their arrangement, it will become obvious that five seem to be clustered together, and six more have settled in that other part of the pool.

Let's call these two groups *verbal* and *nonverbal* gifts. The life of the body will be filled with these, and their use will be divided up between the members.

Five gifts have to do with verbal communication. Six more are nonverbal gifts and are used for the more subtle (and often more powerful!) means of communication through action. In our age of wordiness, it's important for us to know that the verbals are no more important than the others. If you'll examine that list of offices the nominating committee tried to fill tonight, Fred, you'll probably agree that churches have *gone to seed* over verbal gifts!

Part of your frustration may be at this point. It's hard to push all the members over to the part of the well with five coins, and not utilize the other six. Gets crowded over there, doesn't it? By this action, *man's* choices for service in the body life do not balance with God's choices. How sad—many a dear member of the body is trying to minister in a situation requiring a verbal gift he or she does not possess. No wonder it is such a relief to have first cousins visit for the weekend! Even sadder, that same person has been given no recognition by the rest of the body of his or her nonverbal gift. It has rested in the bottom of the well until it is covered with algae.

Before we begin to examine these coins, I want to impress upon you the fantastic power of nonverbal communication! Through the years of pastoring I have spent many hours counseling couples ready to divorce. I began to realize early in the interviews that most of these couples did not openly vent their frustrations. Sometimes a wife would "bite the bullet" and choke on her unhappiness, while the husband freely gave words to his misery. Seldom did I have a troubled couple come to see me who *both* could erupt verbally.

I asked one bullet-biting wife, "When you are angry at your husband, how do you express it? You do not seem to use words. You probably are using *actions* to fight back. Am I right?"

A look of surprise came over her face as she realized exactly how she fought back. "I never realized it before . . . but when I want to *hurt* him, I cook asparagus and liver for his evening meal. He hates them both! It ruins his whole evening."

That husband knew very well the power of *nonverbal* communication. Asparagus and liver were strong enough to tear up his marriage!

If this can be true in a *negative* sense, how much more does it become true in a *positive* situation! The church *must* begin to honor the six nonverbal gifts of its membership.

THE SIX NONVERBALS

1. The Gift of Service

So important is this nonverbal gift that it is placed between the gifts of prophecy and teaching in Romans 12:7. It is described in the New English Bible as the "gift of administration." Unfortunately for Americans, it is hard for us to consider "administration" as having any spiritual side to it. We tend to connect that word to upper-level corporation management.

Literally, the word describes someone who serves as a waiter at tables. It is the word used by unhappy Martha when she said to Jesus (Luke 10:40), "Lord, do you not care that my sister has left me to get on with the *table-waiting* by myself?"

In a wider sense, the word describes the spiritual presence of our Indwelling One, desiring to serve the body needs through us. The word is used for any "discharge of service" in genuine love. In 1 Corinthians 16:15, the entire Stephanas *family* is described as having "laid themselves out to *serve* God's people." Those who possess this gift are filled with delight to be able to serve their brother or sister in the family, knowing that in doing so they are serving Christ! After all, each member of the body is in Christ, and he is the body. All acts of care, all acts of assistance—done with inner longing to serve him—spring from this beautiful coin within the fountain of one's life.

This gift often is the motivation for giving of money to the Lord's people, as well as personal service. How beautifully this comes across in 2 Corinthians 8:1-5: "We must tell you, friends, about the grace of generosity which God has imparted to our congregations in Macedonia. The troubles they have been through have tried them hard, yet in all this they have been so exuberantly happy that from the depths of their poverty they have shown themselves lavishly open-handed. Going to the limit of their resources, as I can testify, and even beyond that limit, they begged us most insistently, and on their own initiative, to be allowed to share in this *generous service* [and there the same Greek word is used to describe this gift!] to their fellow-Christians. And their giving surpassed our expectations; for they gave their very selves, offering them in the first instance to the Lord, but also, under God, to us."

Fred, if there is a "Stephanas family" in your church, you and your nominating committee should share in a prayer of thanksgiving! They should be accepted as a lovely "spiritual" to the body, and honored as much as any pastor or teacher.

It's significant that the Spirit appoints our children to the body at fairly early ages. Do *they* exercise any gifts? As the song says, "Well, here's one!" When young Greg wants to help carry the movie projector for me, I recognize the potential gift of service in him. When little Cheryl wants to help put the silver on the table for the banquet, she should be honored.

Some time ago one of the brothers came to me saying, "Ralph, I barely make enough money to feed the five kids, so my gifts financially are not as lavish as some of the wealthier members. But I have a strong back and arm and I like to work in a garden or a yard. How can I serve?"

Unbeknown to most of the People Who Care, this dear man has trimmed bushes for one of our widows . . . mowed the lawn for a man who was ill for a few weeks . . . and performed many tasks others would have refused. His only request to me was that I not mention him publicly; he wanted God to get all the glory.

This gift is singularly distinguished by a "want to" in the heart. There is no "ought" in the service of such a gifted member of the body. IT JUST ERUPTS!

Over in Joppa Church (Acts 9:36) lived a gazelle-like member named Dorcas. (I really don't know *how* the nominating committee handled her! Maybe back in those days they had a position called "chairman of acts and kindnesses" —but I doubt it.)

At any rate, this Spirit-gifted woman filled her days with acts of kindnesses and charity. So respected was her "spiritual" of helps that, at her death, the poor widows stood "round Peter in a weeping circle." Showing the coats and shirts Dorcas had made for them, they said, "Peter, we can't live without her. She never even asked us for a word of thanks. Noticing our needs, she quietly went home to sew into the night. Then she would appear on our doorstep with clothes for the children. She didn't even wait to stay for lunch. You know, she never did anything spectacular when the body gathered. She could not teach or sing. But no one was hugged more often than our Dorcas! We widows nearly put callouses on her cheeks with our holy kisses. How will we *live* without her?"

So respected was the gift of SERVICE in the infant church that *Dorcas was raised from the dead* by Peter! Fred, you won't find that done for any preacher or teacher in the New Testament. Do you understand now why I chose this gift as the *first* coin to examine?

As we think together, we will begin to understand that the various *offices* of the body—like the office of a deacon, for example—require certain combinations of gifts to be found in the lives of those elected. How many times we elect a member of the body to serve us in an area where a "spiritual" is lacking. How often we suffer because we don't honor the "spirituals" which must exist outside the structure of tradition-bound programs.

Such a lovely coin is the gift of Service! It can be found in male, female, educated, uneducated, young, old, slave, or freeman. Why, it just pops up anywhere! What it *does*, non-verbally, speaks more eloquently than ten thousand silver-tongued orators, all standing in a row.

2. The Gift of Giving

Romans 12:8 describes a gift in these words: "If you give to charity, give with all your heart." The word for *giving* used here describes a man quite deliberately parting with something in his possession, so that a change of ownership is produced. This, says Paul, is to be done "in singleness of mind." The entire operation of this "spiritual" has a note of *abandonment* in it.

42

The most beautiful expression of this gift in use is found in Acts 4:32, where we are told, "Not a man of them claimed any of his possessions as his own, but everything was held in common." Verses 34-35, "They had never a needy person among them, because all who had property in land or houses [*continually*] sold it, [*continually*] brought the proceeds of the sale, and laid the money at the feet of the apostles; it was then distributed to any who stood in need."

Those in that body exercised the gift of giving. At different times, as different members of the body had need, they were *moved by the Spirit* to sell possessions and distribute them through the apostles. This passage does not teach that community-property arrangement had taken place in that church. Each person owned his own property, but the Spirit was obeyed when he moved individuals to share. This is made plain by the comment Peter made to Ananias in 5:4: "While it [the land] remained, did it not remain yours? When it was turned into money, was it not still at your own disposal?" No communal idea here!

That's where the impact of this chapter comes for us believers today. The awareness of the body life was so strong that men *voluntarily* gave their wealth to other members of the congregation. Doing it through the apostles cut the "ego trip" out of the activity. Truly the gifts came from the motion of the Holy Spirit. No one knew who had given what to whom.

The kind of sharing required by this gift is *impossible* apart from the working within of the Spirit! Truly, one possesses a "grace gift" who allows his valuables to flow freely from his hands to others, with no strings attached.

Fred, a number of writers on the "spirituals" single out this gift as limited to those who are able to make and use money to the glory of God. Their reasoning goes that God has smiled upon a select few among the body, and has put them to making money. The capacity to get rich, it follows, is their "spiritual."

Balderdash!

There's nothing wrong with being "wealthy." It's true

43

that a man is to "put aside and keep by him a sum in proportion to his gains" every Sunday (1 Cor. 16:2) . . . but the King James misses the Greek text entirely when it adds, "as *God* hath prospered him." It just doesn't say that.

The importance of the gift of giving is not centered upon the *amount* of wealth a man has accumulated. The significance is in the matter of Spirit-led *faith giving* . . . that is, draining my assets to help another brother, because I firmly believe that God is continually supplying my needs, and he is going to replenish my account.

No more beautiful illustration of this gift has ever come my way than the story Isobel S. Kuhn tells in her lovely book, *In the Arena* (Moody, 1958).

During her lean years in the 1920's as a China-bound missionary student at the Moody Bible Institute, Dr. Page, veteran missionary, took her to a bank. She was astonished when he laid $100 on the counter and opened an account in her name! Her account of her reaction to his generosity is told in the chapter entitled "Obstacles" (p. 29):

"I often wondered how a poor China Inland Mission missionary could find $100.00 to give away all of a sudden like that. Maybe a relative had died and left them a legacy. Some twenty years later when on a furlough I met Dr. Page and decided to ask him. By this time, having been a CIM missionary myself for nearly two decades, I knew that that gift was really wonderful. So I reminded him of it and asked where he got it—was it a legacy?

"I will never forget how he laughed! He threw back his head and just laughed till he cried. 'No, Isobel,' he said, wiping the hilarious tears away. 'I remember it perfectly. We didn't have any legacy. We just emptied our bank account, that was all. We figured that we were old-timers in the life of faith and you were just beginning. It would be easier for us to trust the Lord. A legacy? Oh-ho-ho,' and off he went laughing again."

This is one "spiritual" that every member of the body should enjoy to the fullest! The maturity of the believer will increase the measure of faith and obedience involved in using it, but a babe in the body can exercise it. All members have this gift.

Thinking through the full meaning of this has led me to an entirely new concept of stewardship, which has been the basis of my teaching about giving to the body at West Memorial for nearly five years. I know, Fred, that some will disagree with me . . . but *I do not teach tithing in any form whatsoever!* Our dear body has understood that God is not interested in the AMOUNT we give; he is only interested in WHO STARTED IT! If my *ego* decides that I have made a lot of money this year, and I should give 50 percent to the Lord, I just don't believe God is impressed at all. The crucial issue has to do with that coin in the well. If a man is directed by the *Spirit* to give some amount—regardless of its percentage of total income—it will be exactly the amount God ordered. To make my decision on any other basis is to make giving legalistic and mechanical. How in the earth can a man grow in grace, year by year, and continue to give only a *tenth* of his income? Besides, even a cursory examination of the Old Testament tithe will show it was not 10 percent, but more like 23 1/3 percent!

I shall never forget an evening service when we had our time called "body life." This is just an informal time when anyone in the body, young or old, can share anything in his or her heart. One of our young men stood up and said, "Well, the Lord is teaching me *something!* Saturday I came over to paint our TOUCH sign on the freeway. On the way home, I wrecked my car. I'm just waiting to see how the Lord will provide a way for me to get my wife and me to our jobs this week."

Instantly, a pair of keys to a brand new Oldsmobile came sailing across the room towards him! Another brother said, "Use mine until yours gets fixed."

The impact came for me Thursday of that week, when I had a lunch date with the owner of the Olds. I met him at the store he runs in Houston. He had been borrowing cars from his employees to get around in during business hours, and his dear wife was driving him to and from his place of business morning and evening. His gift of giving had caused him inconvenience, but he never mentioned it. That Olds had come from the Spirit.

"I offer so that a change of ownership is produced . . . with singleness of mind!" Those who exercise this gift may be children, adults, men without jobs, men with large bankrolls.

One of my favorite jokes is the one about two men who met after years of separation. One said to the other, "How's your wife?" After a moment's hesitation, the other replied, "*Compared to what?*"

There is an absurdity in the concepts of being "rich" or being "poor." Compared to *what*? To one man, wealth is a Cadillac instead of a . . . . (you fill in the blank!). To another, it's a concrete floor instead of a dirt floor. To still another, it's *having* a floor.

The gift of giving is not a natural act; it's the *supernatural* moving of the Holy Spirit to lead us to share by faith what he dictates. It's based on the faith that God will supply all my needs, from his own treasury.

3. The Gift of Leadership

This third of the nonverbal gifts is described in the latter part of Romans 12:8: "If you are a leader, exert yourself to lead." Note that this is not describing an *office*, but a "spiritual." Paul admonishes in 1 Thessalonians 5:12, "We beg you, brothers, to acknowledge those who are working so hard among you, and in the Lord's fellowship are your *leaders* and counsellors." The body life is emphasized by the phrase "in the Lord's fellowship."

How does one distinguish between the *natural* capacity to be an executive of great *talent*, and the "spiritual" called *leadership*? A part of that answer has to do with the source of motivation in the person. There is a great difference in the activity of one who is seeking to meet the needs of the people who are around him, and another who is seeking to serve the Head of the body.

A person who leads others through an aggressive disposition, unusual ability to "put things together," and a willingness to work long hours, can be president of any large corporation. He functions on the philosophy that he has a job because there are people with problems "who need a partner." He sets long-range goals, prepared "PERT" charts, checks "bogies," and runs sales conferences. He motivates others by inspiring, educating, and setting a personal example.

When he finishes leading others, he can stand back and say, "I know exactly why this has happened. It was my elbow grease and brain brawn. I know why it happened—and so does the Board of Directors!"

His motivation will usually be quite complicated. Seldom is it money. Often it may be power. Occasionally it may just be a desire to prove that because Dad was a bum does not mean he must be one, also. Contrast such motivation with the "spiritual" of leadership.

The gift of leadership will also demand all the physical, mental, and emotional parts of a person to be dedicated to the work. But that *work* will be what the Head of the body has commanded. The leadership gift is recognized in a member of the body as he demonstrates his capacity to be totally obedient to the Head. The leadership gift does not have to do with goals and committees; it involves identifying the members who stand tall and say, "I have been with God. He has dealt with my spirit. He has given us his mandate. This is the command of the Lord!"

Of paramount importance is the capacity of this one to ask in prayer again and again, "Lord, since you are not interested in *what* we *do*, have you any orders for the body?" Then, like Moses, he comes down from the mountain. The body recognizes his authority to lead. His face is shining with the reflection of the One who has spoken to him. His commitment to the Lord's calling is as deep as his heartbeat. Murmurings, disappointments, and feeling alone will not slow him down. He leads others not on the basis of talents, but from a total obedience to the call of God.

How desperately our generation of Christians needs men and women of such stature! Blessed indeed is the body which can number many who know how to pray, to be quiet and listen to the Head, and to move ahead with absolute conviction that *God* started what they are doing.

The leader who "serves his people" will walk like a prophet. He must serve the Head, and be prepared for whatever cost this might require.

In Acts 13 we find the congregation, including their prophets and teachers, "offering worship to the Lord." They had erased the blackboard of their own goals, plans, and strategies. They had come before their Head for fellowship and to listen to him speak. In that time of quietness, "the Holy Spirit said, 'Set Barnabas and Saul apart for me, to do the work to which I have called them.' Then, after further fasting and prayer, they laid their hands on them and let them go."

In a prayer meeting of that congregation, the first missionary society was born and the first missionaries were sent out. Long range and short range goals were now possible. Leaders were appointed by the Spirit for the work of that body. Those simple Christians of Antioch had an outreach to hundreds of distant villages and great cities. From their "worship to the Lord," a mission so gigantic was born that all present *knew* God had started it! Not a man among them would have had the courage to propose such an enormous goal. Only an omnipotent Head would be capable of doing so.

The Lord's body should not have any place for volunteers for positions of leadership! Every single leader it has must be one who has been *drafted* for his task. Jesus, our leader, shared the pattern for all who are given the gift of leadership: "As thou hast sent me into the world, I have sent them into the world, and for their sake I now concentrate myself, that they too may be consecrated [*set apart for service*] by the truth" (John 17:18-19).

Paul tells us that God does not recognize the personal distinctions made among men, which put some into places of prominent reputation (Gal. 2:6). Sad indeed in this day is the manner by which the church finds itself electing men of prominent reputation, who often actually campaign like politicians for their office.

48

Contrast this with the work of the Spirit! Martin
Luther's mantle did not come from any pope, nor did the
leadership of Charles Haddon Spurgeon come from office
seeking. Billy Sunday was placed by the Spirit before the
American public as surely as Paul was sent to Macedonia.
Revered indeed is our own generation's Billy Graham, appointed to be an evangelistic preacher apart from any board.
Most hallowed is the memory of George W. Truett, who heard
the command of the Head and became his leader of body
parts.

Should not every *leader* within body life be recognized
for his or her "spiritual" in advance of election or appointment to ministry? *Is it too late to start?*

4. Helping Others in Distress

The Greek word used in Romans 12:8, "If you are *helping others in distress*, do it cheerfully," is sometimes translated by the English words "compassion" or "console." It is
placed among the nonverbal gifts, because it is not referring to
the ability to counsel with people. As Thayer's lexicon explains, the word means *"to feel sympathy with the misery of
another, especially such sympathy as manifests itself in act,
less frequently in word."*

Now, Fred, how in the world do you console *cheerfully?*
What could be *worse* than a friend who comes over to sympa-
thize with you when you are miserable—and whistles tunes
into your ear? Job's buddies were at least smarter than that!

Here, however, is precisely the point of this nonverbal
gift. Only a fellow member of the body can help me in my
moment of deepest distress, for my unbelieving friend does
not share the blessed hope with me!

Anyone can come over and sit by my side when I am
grieving over the death of a loved one, and weep with me. Indeed, I have seen hired wailers who do exactly *that*—for a fee—
in the Far East. There *is* a certain comfort in such an act, or
people would not be willing to put out money for the service.
But it only provides the comfort of feeling I am not *alone* in
my sorrow. There is provided no hope for the future.

When one possesses this gift, there is the capacity to communicate—nonverbally—the assurance that God is on the throne! This inner flow of the Spirit brings the solace and comfort of hope.

Some people have this gift, and some do not. Paul did not seem to exercise it with John Mark, nor did he particularly show it in his relationships with Peter or the Corinthian church. Many in the body today simply feel uncomfortable, unable to function adequately, in those situations where the gift is needed.

Some months ago a dear member of our Houston fellowship who demonstrates many other "spirituals" called me. A friend had just received a death-call, and was weeping profusely. Our member said, "Ralph, I'm all thumbs! Please come right over." This lack of ease in the situation was caused by her not having one of the coins in the fountain. How beautiful it is when we recognize its presence in one another, and feel free to call upon those who have it. Not all do!

There is another facet of this gift, expressed by the use of the same Greek word in Jude 22-23: "There are some doubting souls who need your *pity* [compassion, consolation]; snatch them from the flames and save them." Here is a nonverbal gift which is used in the evangelistic task of sharing Jesus with unbelievers. Indeed, it is described as precisely the gift which will best reveal the Head to some types of unbelievers. Cheerfully helping others in distress is an atomic bomb of a gift!

A few years ago, members of our body worked in a half-way house for heroin addicts. The director of the ministry was an exjunkie, and his gift of leadership from the Lord to conduct this work attracted others. Those in our body who worked with him had no previous experience with drug addicts. They were given only one assignment: *cheerfully help those in distress.*

Carl, Bob, and others discovered that heroin withdrawal causes days—and weeks—of intense pain, similar to the flu. Aching bones, nausea, diarrhea, stomach cramps, vomiting . . . hour after hour! The second floor of the house contained sleeping quarters for the women, with couples and single men downstairs. On occasion, as many as thirty adults were in the miseries of withdrawal.

Again and again I would drive over to the house to check on our members, and the hurting bodies. Never have I felt the reality of this passage in Jude as in that situation . . . "*snatch them from the flames and save them.*"

They are *in* "hell"; they didn't need it *preached* to them. They *knew* the wages of sin; they didn't need to be reminded of them. Those "doubting souls" needed only what our folks took to them: simply the nonverbalized *gift of pity*.

Like fixing a cup of coffee.

Or sitting down in the same room, and saying nothing until a junkie felt up to "rapping."

And, as one of our gals did, combing out the snarls from the hair of a girl who was too sick to care anymore.

That holy "spiritual" evangelized more eloquently than any sermon. It caused those addicts to begin to show up on Sundays to worship with us. How beautiful it was to see a precious member of the body go up to her exprostitute (and sometimes not so "ex"!) friend—and give her a bear hug.

And then they came to Jesus. Tony. Bonny. Oh! How it hurts to include Joe Ike, who had his picture taken with me for *People* magazine some years ago. Thank God for Bob and Carl, who just *pitied*; because of his grace flowing through that half-way house, Joe Ike received Christ one day.

Later, he was riding in the front seat with another junkie. When the car shot under the back of a semi-truck, Joe Ike was decapitated.

At his funeral, the same coin from the fountain was manifested in the "other" way. Now it was our turn to share with his wife, who had prayed with me one day at that house of pain to receive Christ. The "spiritual" of consolation was our gift to her.

Is it not significant for the body to have some awareness of the names of those members who possess this lovely gift, Fred? After all, some of the offices require this coin to be in the fountain.

5. The Gift of Faith

"Another, by the same Spirit, is granted faith" (1 Cor. 12:9). Have you ever noticed the significant comment about faith in Romans 12:3? We are taught there that God doles out to each of us a *measure* of faith. In other words, God measures out a specific *quantity* of faith to each believer—and some are given a greater measure than others. Recognition of those members of the body who have the coin of faith enables a congregation to have spiritual vision. You might call this nonverbal gift the "eyes of the body." The retinas of the eyes of faith can discern heavenly realities before they become a part of earth's realities.

The obvious reason why all members of the body do not have the same measure of faith is because some parts of the body do not need as much of it for their function. Arnold Toynbee has commented on the nature of man in society in a way that illustrates this.

He points out that there is a balance among men who are divided into the creative personalities and the mimicists. The creative person is one who can build a castle in the air. He sees something before it actually exists, and can describe it clearly enough to excite others to build it.

However, the creative person often lacks the durable quality of the mimicist, who is far more capable of putting the castle together, brick by brick. By the time the walls of the castle are being erected, the creative person has moved on to something else. No matter; the mimicist is committed to the castle-building, and will not stop until it is completed. But don't ask the mimicist to dream about another project! It would scare him to death.

One is an architect; the other is a contractor. In the body of Christ, some have the ability to dream dreams and see visions. They "give substance to our hopes, and make us certain of realities we do not see" (Heb. 11:1). Others in the body have the body task of solidifying the realities.

As one person has described it, "Faith is believing that something *is* so, when it *isn't* so, so that it will *be* so." Simple trust that God is going to do what he has covenanted to do is the foundation for such faith.

Charlie is a member of our body who has caused the rest of us to acknowledge he has the gift of faith. After being out of work for two years and spending several thousand dollars trying to go back to work in the computer field, he came to see me. God had given him a dream! It involved teaching (one of his "spirituals") and sharing with laymen across the nation. His vision astounded me! It was obvious that *he* hadn't started this—he never could have figured it all out. Moreover, he and Inez had felt called to do this ministry just as their life savings, which they had lived on for two years, were depleted.

The next Sunday Charlie said to me, "Ralph, I put $50 in the offering plate today." I suggested that perhaps he should hold on to the modest amount he still had in savings to carry him through the coming lean months. He replied, "I just don't believe the Lord has given me this vision in order to starve us to death! I put my gift into the church today as a faith-act. I believe God will supply our needs, and I am contributing from those earnings in advance."

Right then and there, I knew we had discovered another person in the body who had the faith coin. It was further verified on Tuesday, when he called me so excited he could hardly read the letter which had just arrived. It was from a remote friend, known only casually from a trip made a few months earlier. She told how, in her prayer time, the Lord had impressed upon her the importance of sending a love gift to Charlie and Inez. Enclosed was her check for . . .

FIVE HUNDRED DOLLARS!

For nearly a year now, Charlie has lived by faith. He has flown all over this country teaching TOUCH Basic Training courses, and conducting deeper life conferences.

The entire body has profited from watching his cold-steel faith walk. Many others have stepped out by faith to trust the Lord for situations and things because of the gift Charlie has exhibited for us.

The Giver of the gifts can be depended upon to place the Faith People in each body of Christ. Sometimes it's an aged grandmother; sometimes it's a pastor's wife; sometimes it's a Charlie. Such members are always able to *see the kingdom* [rule, reign] *of God before it touches earth.*

Through the faith gifts in our body, we were led two years ago to vote to build a center for weekday ministries which could also convert for worship and Sunday School space. At the time we voted to go ahead, the expected monthly payments were far beyond the capacity of our weekly income. I knew that the "rule of thumb" for a building cost should limit us to spending no more than 1½ times our annual income. The building was going to cost *six times* that figure!

In all honesty, I felt I needed to caution the men in our planning groups. Their response was, "Pastor, we've prayed this thing through. *God* is the one who started this, and we are moving on with confidence."

The faith of those men was one reason they had been called by the body to serve in the planning groups dealing with funding and designing the new structure. The body voted hilariously on the issue, and swept us into the signed contracts.

And then the faith-gifts became sight-facts! Fifty-five thousand dollars cash was committed in less than ten minutes by a congregation comprised of only 190 men, women, and children. An additional cash flow into the building fund over the next few months increased that figure to $75,000. In that same period of time, the growth of the body began in an unprecedented manner. Offerings quickly doubled, then swelled toward the tripling stage. Our treasurer has just informed me that last month, with all bills paid, the receipts were $1,000 more than our needs!

I'd *like* to say that the *pastor* led the troops into that victory, with his faith-coin held high. The *fact* of the matter is that the eyes were elsewhere. Those of the laity with their sight-gift were like Caleb and Joshua reporting at Kadesh-Barnea. I was a bit like the other spies who came back and . . . uh . . .

. . . uh, pardon me while I do wander in the wilderness!

6. The Gift of Distinguishing True Spirits from False

"Ability to distinguish true spirits from false" (1 Cor. 12:10) is the last of the nonverbal gifts. It provides the protection of the Spirit, sensing and isolating the source of a potential invasion by foreign "spirits." It is a capacity given to some within the body, to be exercised in the guarding of other members.

Ours is a day of fuzzy thinking concerning our ultimate source of truth. Experience has become the source for many doctrines accepted without question in today's church. This can be considered to be a direct attack by Satan upon the authority of the Scriptures! The Jesus People movement of a few years ago has left in its wreckage the idea that "if all else crumbles, just hang on to your *experience* with Christ. No one can take that away from you." That type of mentality has not only bred many false doctrines within Christianity; it has also opened a Pandora's box of "greater" and "greater" non-Christian experiences which have been around for centuries in Hindu thought. In recent days, one of these antichrists has drawn the ex-Jesus people by the scores to the fantastic "light" that can be seen by pressing your fingers into your eyeballs!

Along with this, there is a "fad" rampant today among evangelicals. It has to do with demons. Satan and demons are "bound" by the "blood" and the believer's "authority" out of rooms, meeting halls, and even whole towns. Amateur exorcists sprout up everywhere. At a recent conference, one dear saint was seen "praying demons out of her doorknob" (it kept sticking!) in the hotel hallway. Another brother listened to me teach from Galatians in a small group meeting in a home for over an hour. Finally he said, "I have never heard that teaching before. But I am sure it is true, because just as you entered the room I sealed it off from Satan at the walls and ceiling by covering them with the blood in prayer. Therefore, I *know* you have spoken truth." The inference, of course, was that if he had *not* done so, the exposition of the Scriptures might have had a demonic twist.

I most emphatically do *not* believe that fellow was mani-

festing the "gift of distinguishing true spirits from false!"
Something far more significant in the life of the body is being
described here than that.

Literally, the Greek says this gift consists of a capacity
to *separate*, or *differentiate*, between *"spirits."* It is a capacity that is described as increasing in proportion to the spiritual maturity of the possessor: "But grown men can take solid food; their perceptions are trained by long use to *discrimi-
nate* [same Greek word as in 1 Cor. 12:10] between good
and evil" (Heb. 5:14). In the context of this passage, the
writer is explaining that believers should advance toward maturity. When they do, he indicates, this gift becomes operative.

John seems to verify the importance of growth, dividing
believers into three groups. First, there are the "little children" who are struggling to find victory over the sins of their
past lives. There are also the "young men" who have mastered the evil one. *It is important to notice how that mastery
takes place*: "To you, young men, I have written because you
are strong; *God's word is in you,* and you have mastered the
evil one" (1 John 2:14). Ahah! Maturity does not come
through some clairvoyant capacity, but by the soaking up of
the water of the Word of God. Scripture, our *only* source of
information, is isolated as the focal point of all authority.
Finally, one becomes a "father"—able to reproduce in kind.
Fathers "know him who is and has been from the beginning."

It would seem that this gift of separating the spirits
comes as the believer learns how to rightly separate the Word
of Truth. The knowledge imparted by the holder of this gift
is not some supernatural ability to "sense" demons—or any
other type of spirit—but to apply the sole authority of faith
and practice, THE BIBLE, to test for the truth.

Otherwise, we have the knotty problem on our hands of
a member of the body who piously announces he has the
God-given capacity to sense the presence of evil spirits. He
can "discern" demons of homosexualism, prenatal demons
which were transferred from the ovum of the mother or the
sperm of the father to a fetus. He senses the presence of the

demons of anger, masturbation, obesity, etc. One such clairvoyant announced to an interested audience that he had just
spoken to a demon who had indicated that he had divided
himself into nine parts, and had taken up residence in nine
humans.

WHERE IS THE BIBLICAL AUTHORITY FOR SUCH
A CLAIM?

Paul wrote the great doctrinal summary for Christians of
all ages when he penned the Epistle to the Romans. It is most
significant that he worked meticulously through the problem
of the carnal nature of man, chapter by chapter, and *never
once mentioned demons!*

Of further significance in understanding the nature of
this gift is the study of the word used for "spirits" used in
1 Corinthians 12:10. Shades of meaning for it include:

1. A movement of air, as in the breath of the nostrils.

2. The spirit, the vital life-principle by which the human
body is animated.

3. A spirit higher than man but lower than God, that is,
an angel. Here it is used of demons, or evil spirits, who were
conceived of as inhabiting the bodies of men.

4. The spiritual nature of God, Christ, the Holy Spirit.

5. One in whom a spirit (as in 3) is manifest or embodied; hence, actuated by a spirit, whether divine or demoniacal;
one who either is truly moved by God's Spirit or falsely
boasts that he is.

This summary, taken from Thayer's lexicon, helps to
understand the scope of the use of this gift of differentiating.
Nothing in the context limits this gift to (5), although it is
certainly included in the extent of it. Significant is the fact
that all the gifts are to be exercised exclusively within and on
behalf of the body life. They are not practiced within the
body by an itinerant; they are the *permanent* manifestations
of the indwelling Spirit. The body looks to the members who
possess this gift to assist in discerning a threat to its spiritual
life from:

1. *A human spirit who desires to share in the life of the
body, and who is not joined to it by the Head.* This is the rea-

son for Jude's letter. (It, incidentally, is a marvelous example of the proper use of this spiritual gift.) He writes, "My friends, . . . it became urgently necessary to write at once and appeal to you to join the struggle in defense of the faith, the faith which God entrusted to his people once and for all. It is in danger from *certain persons* who have wormed their way in, the very men whom *Scripture* long ago marked down for the doom they have incurred" (v. 3-4). His use of the gift was against *certain persons*. His method of discerning their presence as a foreign body was through use of *Scripture*.

"Their dreams lead them to *defile the body*, to flout authority, and to insult celestial beings" (v. 8). *His purpose for attacking them was his concern for the defiled body life.* This was also the great prayer burden of Paul, who shared with the elders of the congregation of Ephesus: "Keep watch over yourselves and over all the flock of which the Holy Spirit has given you charge . . . I know that when I am gone, savage wolves will come in among you and will not spare the flock. Even from your own body there will be men coming forward who will distort the truth to induce the disciples to break away and follow them" (Acts 20:28-30).

This suggests a second threat from . . .

2. *A human spirit who is within the body life, and who is contaminating it with willful sinning.* Ananias and Saphira were two such spirits who were called home quickly. Paul referred to a man in 1 Corinthians 5:5 who was within the body, and ordered him "consigned to Satan for the destruction of the body, so that his *spirit* may be saved on the Day of the Lord." Discerning the spirit of human rebellion and willful disobedience in my brother, says John (1 John 5:16-17), is a matter to be left for the Head to punish. We are not even supposed to waste our time *praying* for him: he is going to face the judgment of God for his acts!

3. *One in whom a spirit (demon) is manifest or embodied.* Multiple instances of using the gift of discerning those trapped in this situation are recorded for us in the book of Acts.

The coming of Jesus Christ to the earth was marked by a

plethora of demonic outburst! A study of church history shows that it subsided in the centuries that followed. As we draw closer to the return of Christ, the obvious presence of Satan and his legions must be reckoned with. Blind indeed is the congregation which cannot see the reality of the situation.

The problem is that those who have moved into this arena have left others of us behind, still searching the Scriptures! Of great danger is the experience-centered authority of much of the literature currently selling like hotcakes on this subject. Are we *really* so blind as to build a system of dealing with demons based upon what *they* supposedly *say to the exorciser,* rather than from the clear statements of Scripture? A careful scrutiny of the writers in this area will validate, in too many cases, that this is precisely what is taking place.

It is a doctrinally dangerous thing to exceed the teachings of Paul, who states flatly in Romans that "De Debble *Didn't Make Us Do It!"* My personal rebellion against God is the source of my sin. Scripture nowhere teaches that homosexualism, for example, is the result of demon possession: it is clearly the result of God giving up profane men, letting the due course of their rebellion take place. What could be clearer than that in the first chapter of his Epistle? Nothing further is taught. Nothing more is to be added.

In summary: this gift can be expected to occur in the members of the body who are mature students of the Scriptures. It will be founded upon their ability to apply biblical doctrines to problemed people, and not upon some mystical capacity to sense the "vibrations" of evil spirits. Spirits, of whatever classification, are to be discerned by the power of the Scriptures, not the clairvoyance of an individual.

Those who have this "spiritual" are vital to the protection of the body. The Giver can be relied upon to place some with this capacity in every body.

Perhaps the most direct passage in the New Testament to use as a guideline for the use of this gift is 1 John 4:1-3: "But do not trust any and every spirit, my friends; test the spirits, to see whether they are from God, for among those who have gone out into the world there are many prophets falsely inspired. This is how we may recognize the Spirit of God: every spirit which acknowledges that Jesus Christ has come in the flesh is from God, and every spirit which does not thus acknowledge Jesus is not from God. This is what is meant by 'Antichrist'; you have been told that he was to come, and here he is, in the world already!"

The implication here is that a false spirit will deny the incarnation of the Deity. The spirit of antichrist referred to here is the false spirit who will later possess antichrist.

The discerning of spirits leads to the matter of biblical truth in dealing with them as they threaten the body life. Here, a guideline entitled "Fools rush in where angels fear to tread" is given by Jude 9: "When the archangel Michael was in debate with the devil . . . he did not presume to condemn him in insulting words, but said, 'May the Lord rebuke you!' " Like the 1 John 5:16 passage, this indicates that the Head of the body has reserved some "spirituals" to himself, and the members should recognize this fact. He is our exorciser!

7
Some More Coins

Fred, as you and your committee work to nominate people to positions in the church, you may begin to feel that some of the functions of your job description may be presuming upon the work which should be left to the Head and the Spirit. I'm going to let you struggle a while over that problem!

In the meantime, let's move on and examine . . .

FIVE VERBAL GIFTS

1. The Gift of Prophecy

"The gift of inspired utterance . . . in proportion to a man's faith" (Rom. 12:6); "another has the gift of prophecy" (1 Cor. 12:10). These two passages are but an introduction to the many, many verses which deal with this "spiritual." The first question that pops into our mind about this gift has to do with the *foretelling* aspect which is sometimes connected to it. Does it refer to one who can be expected to stand in a spiritual swoon in the service and speak words of truth that come from God to the body?

In the Old Testament, the Hebrew equivalent of this word is related to the word for *mouth*. Prophecy was seen as the telling-forth of the *words* of God and the *wisdom* of God. The man involved was a mouthpiece through whom God spoke truth. The prophet spoke out what God provided: he was a *mouthpiece*.

Regardless of the item of *foretelling*, the prophet was

always a *forthteller*. He did not always foretell. Sometimes he pronounced judgment on sin. Sometimes he pointed memories to past wickedness, and warned that God is not mocked. And sometimes he *was* a foreteller, but that item was not—even in the Old Testament—the focal point of the prophet's work. He was sent to straighten out people.

In the New Testament, the gift of prophecy does not change. As the gift of faith is an eye in the body, so the gift of prophecy is a mouthpiece in the body. It refers to one who *tells forth* the *Word of God*.

What is the source, or what are the sources, for the words to be spoken by the person exercising the gift of prophecy? Included in the possibilities would be:

1. Scripture
2. Trances
3. Dreams
4. Visions

What criteria exist to decide how many of all the possible sources are authentic?

To begin with, this is a "spiritual" with a purpose. Prophecy is the manifestation of the Spirit through a person "for some useful purpose." We may rule out, then, those situations where prophetic utterances serve no useful purpose. Those who seek for thrills will receive no sign "except that of the prophet Jonah." The inspired utterance will be *practical*!

Second, crucial to our conclusion is the matter of revelation: has God given us a complete, or an incomplete, revelation in Jesus Christ? If, further, the Scriptures do *not* record the total truth about Christ and what God wants man to know, there will be a need for continuing information from him to supplement the Bible record.

But the Scriptures contain voluminous chapters of *foretelling* passages. They stretch past our day to ages to come. So broad are these "foretellings" that Bible students have occupied themselves for two millenniums scrutinizing them. Does it seem possible that they left out some important detail, which will be revealed to a small congregation in some obscure town by a member of the body who speaks forth from a vision, dream, or trance? If this is the case, would God withhold this important information from the rest of the human race? *The fact that the Bible has remained unchanged for 1900 years answers these questions!* There is no incomplete revelation. If there were, those like Joseph Smith who try to add *The Book of Mormon* would be earnestly sought after by main stream Christianity. Such writings and prophecies have cropped up century after century. They have been *universally* rejected as being unworthy of inclusion in inspired Scripture. There is only the finished work of the cross, and the completed fact of the Canon! This is our only authority!

In earlier years, God spoke through the prophets in "fragmentary and varied fashion." His final revelation, and the written record of it, needs no last-minute Sunday night additions by a foreteller: it "cuts more keenly than any two-edged sword. . . . It sifts the purposes and thoughts of the heart" (Heb. 4:12).

Let us agree, then, that the exerciser of this mouthpiece gift *will foretell*: by reading and expounding the *Scriptures which foretell*. But he will *also* expound hundreds of other chapters in the Bible that deal with God's relationships to man. And—thank you, Lord—he will do it with the certitude that he has *all there is: there isn't any more to come.*

Having settled that thorny question, Fred, let's move on to reaffirm that the gift of prophecy is not limited to the "Reverend" in the pulpit. Many within the fellowship will be discovered who can open the Word and tell forth the wisdom of God. They can be expected to be directed by the Spirit to preaching ministries other than the one reserved for a pastor.

Remember Philip?

His gift of prophecy enabled the Spirit to use him to help a eunuch in a chariot by a river. The poor fellow was bogged down in Isaiah until "Philip began . . . from this passage . . . the good news of Jesus" (Acts 8:35). Philip was a man with the gift of prophecy, but he was not a pastor of a church at this time.

Fred, it is a wonderful thing to have a pastor who recognizes himself to be an equipper of the saints, and who will develop to the fullest those with the latent gift of prophecy in the body. Their development is, according to Romans 12:6, in direct ratio to the amount of faith possessed. Prophecy will always require faith to operate. The deeper that faith, the deeper the prophecy. Some men have faith so great that they expound the word to depths that boggle the mind! These men are revered by all.

2. The Gift of Teaching

"A teacher should employ his gift in teaching" (Rom. 12:7). Fred, let's talk a little about those teachers in your Sunday School who show such obvious signs of half-heartedness. The study of the Scriptures concerning "teaching" would seem to indicate they have no reason to be given a class. Perhaps, however, resentment should not be focused upon *them*, but upon a *system* which has drifted so far away from the Word that members of the body are being encouraged to function without concern for their lack of "spirituals."

Of one thing we may be certain: the giving of this gift to the body will not be limited to a few. Jesus' Commission requires a large number to be involved in teaching: "He said, 'Full authority in heaven and on earth has been committed to me. Go forth therefore and make all nations my disciples; baptize men everywhere in the name of the Father and the Son and the Holy Spirit, and *teach them to observe all that I have commanded you*. And be assured, I am with you always, to the end of time' " (Matt. 28:18-20).

"Making all nations disciples" requires one group of gifts. The act of water baptism is a point-in-time act, witnessing to the receiving of the Head and being joined to the body. The gift of teaching requires a large number who possess a special relationship to the Head and to the converts. It requires the teacher to be a "middle person."

One who teaches others must be in the continual process of being taught by the Holy Spirit. He receives, so he is qualified to give. John 14:6 gives the pattern: "The Holy Spirit whom the Father will send in my name, will *teach you* everything, and will call to mind all that I have told you."

64

The coin must be seen in relation to the fountain. The divine presence of the Holy Spirit must be the teacher of the teacher!

Kittel's *Theological Dictionary* brought up an obscure passage in the Old Testament that helped me understand this, Fred. Let me share it with you.

Back in Numbers 3:1, the sons of Aaron are also referred to as the sons of Moses. The reason behind this had to do with the importance of the teacher in a student's life in that period of time. While Aaron fathered his sons physically, their instruction in the knowledge of Jehovah came from *Moses*: therefore, he was considered to have *given them birth* through introducing them to the Law.

What a beautiful picture of the relationship between the Holy Spirit and one possessing the gift of teaching! He is the Father of all who teach.

Further, both of the Gospel passages above agree on the *content* of the teaching. It involves "all Jesus has told us." Spirit-given content centers primarily upon expounding and exhorting, rather than a cold transmission of facts. "What he taught us to observe" is infinitely more than a set of rules. It is a way to live under the reign of God. Rote sharing of information will not get this job done! We may be sure this was the focal point for Paul in Acts 28:31, where he is described as "teaching the facts about the Lord Jesus Christ quite openly." His manner of moving beyond the *facts* to the *spirit* is exhibited in Acts 20:31: "Remember how for three years, night and day, I never ceased to counsel each of you, and how I wept over you."

Some years ago, a woman came to see me in the little office of the Valley Baptist Church in Middletown, Pennsylvania. She said, "Pastor, my heart is broken!" Throwing down a list of names before me, she went on: "This is the list of girls I am teaching every Sunday morning. Six out of the fourteen are not close to their Lord. Three more are not yet Christians. Pastor, they are like a ton of lead pressing upon my heart! I can't stand the hurt inside!"

Fred, I wish you could have heard her teach those girls!

She never arrived late. She was never unprepared. She needed no prodding from the Superintendent. She had a gift of teaching, and she possessed one essential quality that only the Spirit gives: her motive for teaching was to see the lives of those girls *totally transformed* by the power of God. She wanted to settle for nothing less than the "rebirth" of those fourteen girls. She went through the agonies of birth pains, even as did Paul when he wrote to the Galatians, "For my children you are, and I am in travail with you over again until you take the shape of Christ."

Gradually, those girls were shaped. I would see them run up to that precious teacher as children would run to their own mother. Blessed ones they were: they had both an "Aaron" and a "Moses" in their lives.

A study of the Greek word for "teaching" brings up a significant point about all this. It involves the use of that word in a certain context for over two and a half centuries before Christ came to earth. About that long before, the rabbis had translated the Old Testament into the more widely read Greek language. In this translation, they used the Greek word for "teaching" about a hundred times. It was, consequently, a word with a very special meaning to a Jew by the time Jesus came to walk among men.

To the non-Jew, "teaching" meant something limited to the sphere of the mind. Not so to a Hebrew! He considered the very use of this word to involve *the imparting of the revealed will of God, and instructions which ordered the relationships between God and man.*

To him, it meant nothing else! This special meaning of the word was related to scores of passages like 2 Chronicles 17:9: "They taught in Judah, having with them the book of the law of the Lord; they went round the cities of Judah, teaching the people."

This same concept carries itself over into the Greek word in the New Testament. Jesus is seen primarily as a teacher. He *sat down*—the posture of one who declared the Scriptures—taught them. He declared the book of the law, beginning in his twelfth year. And he did not hesitate to add to it his own teachings, summarized forever in Matthew 5-7.

He then spent nearly three years living with his students, demonstrating the application of the Sermon on the Mount in every conceivable life situation. The teaching involved mountain and lake experiences, prayer and confrontations with the devil, doubt and faith problems.

To the end, the students had not passed their final exams. The final act of teaching for Christ was the Calvary road. He taught not only with tears, as did Paul, but also *with his blood*. He taught with the resurrection. He taught with the fish by the lake. He taught with the scars in his hands and side. His goal was not the communication of information, but the shaping of lives. He taught by his very life observed! These men would never be the same again. They would be so shaken by his teaching that they would go to martyr's graves rather than compromise again with doubt and fear.

Such was the pattern set by the Head of the body. When his Spirit presses the coin of teaching into the life of a member of that body, he will be marked by the use of the method of the Master. That method involves:

1. Total obedience within the life of the teacher.
2. A thirst for prayer.
3. A deep knowledge of the Word.
4. The capacity to expound the Scriptures in depth.
5. A great commitment to the students, involving the transformation of their lives.
6. A life which documents the truths being taught, and sets forth the pattern for applying them to everyday situations.

Roma Bader was that kind of a teacher to me in childhood. When I was promoted from the Primary to the Junior Department, I was the nastiest preacher's kid that has ever lived. The next-nastiest was a deacon's kid named Billy. We were partners in mayhem!

We were sent to be a part of "MISS" Bader's class. She was nearly as old as our mothers, and we decided (for no good reason!) to give her the hardest time possible. We spitballed and whispered our way through that first month with her, delighting in totally destroying any possible learning situation. She stayed with us, loving all the way. Finally, she announced a class party.

Billy and I went for only one reason: our mothers made us! Early in the party, we arranged to deliberately plop her cake into the bowl of punch. This was followed up by sneering at her first parlor game! (At my present level of maturity, I wonder how *I* might now react to brats like that. . . .)

Roma sat down with us. I now know her heart was breaking. She asked us what we'd rather play than her parlor games. Billy and I looked at each other, and our eyes said, "What's the meanest thing we can make her do?"

I said, "Let's all try to climb the cliff at Cascade Park." (My father wouldn't let me go near the place!) She excused herself, changed her lovely dress for hiking clothes, and took us to do exactly that! We realized as the climb took place that she was driving herself to the place of exhaustion, but she would not give up. Bruised and torn, she led us in climbing that bluff.

I cannot ever remember feeling more ashamed of myself! Her love kept reaching to us in spite of every rebuff we could conjure. And so that was the year . . . and she was the teacher . . . when Christ began to form himself in a significant way in my young life. She laid foreign missions on my heart. She taught me how to witness. She got me to memorizing Scripture. She taught me about prayer.

She went through birthpangs for me! As much as any teacher of my life, she is my "Moses." And then God called her to New York City to be a missionary to the Hebrew people. My rejection of her was *literally child's play* in contrast to what she faced on the Lower East Side. How I thank God for her lifetime of demonstrating the gift of teaching in its purest, holiest form!

A person like that stands out in the body like a . . . *healed* thumb! It wasn't hard for others to become aware that she had the gift of teaching.

The body should not *tolerate* the appointing of any person to teach who does not exhibit these qualifications. Things might have to get worse before they get better if this policy is put into effect . . . but until the line is drawn, those who have this gift will have no real encouragement to discover it. As long as the congregation will *tolerate* mediocrity, they will *get* mediocrity. Such a congregation and its teachers truly deserve each other!

Fred, there is a simple rule we must apply to correct problems like this one. I love to share it with pastors when we talk together about the problems of the church. I have likened this rule to the way an oak tree handles the problem of its dead leaves. They just go on clinging to the branches until spring comes. The stately oak makes no attempt to remove them by violent action. They are dead, that's true—but in the wintertime they aren't hurting anything. When new life comes to the tree, little fresh green shoots appear. Soon the pressure of them causes the dead leaves to drop silently, without argument, to the ground. The fresh leaves, green and productive, cause the oak to increase in size and strength. Change within the church should happen in the same manner. Let the old alone. Just begin now to apply the new truth, letting it shape the present and the future. The rest will be removed by attrition.

The Head will see to that!

3. The Gift of Wise Speech

4. The Gift of Putting the Deepest Knowledge into Words

These two gifts may be a bit confusing at first, since they sound like they might be referring to the same thing. They are both mentioned in 1 Corinthians 12:8: "One man, through the Spirit, has the gift of wise speech, while another, by the power of the same Spirit, can put the deepest knowledge into words." Paul has gone to great pains here to explain that these *are* separate coins, and that they will be found in separate parts of the body. The gifts are given for practical functions, and so they will be tied to specific forms of ministry.

The "spiritual" of *wise speech* is described by a Greek word meaning "broad and full intelligence." This word is used in Matthew 12:42 concerning a man who is renowned for this gift: Solomon. His knowledge of God's ways made it possible to exhibit great wisdom in dealing with knotty problems. (Remember the way he handled the two women who both claimed to be the mother of the same baby?) This same gift is attributed to Joseph in Acts 7:10, and caused him to be appointed chief administrator for Egypt.

The Holy Spirit carries this gift from its source: the Lamb that was slain, described in Revelation 5:12 as possessing "all power and wealth, *wisdom* and might." It flows from the Head of the body, and is directed toward the problems of men." In him lie hidden all God's treasures of *wisdom* and *knowledge*" (Col. 2:3). *Both the coins we are now considering are IN HIM!*

The gift of wisdom is specifically required as a prerequisite for the Seven, probably the first deacons in the Jerusalem church (Acts 6:3): "Look out seven men of good reputation from your number, men full of the Spirit *and of wisdom*." The prerequisite for the prerequisite was that they be Spirit-full men. One absolutely cannot have the latter unless he has the former! In addition, the remark is made in a following verse that of the Seven, Stephen also contained the gift of faith.

Wise speech is also needed to relate properly towards those who are not in the body life (Col. 4:5). In that same letter, it is described as necessary for those who teach and preach (3:16). It is needed for a balanced Christian life, according to James, who teaches: "If any of you falls short in *wisdom*, he should ask God for it and it will be given him, for God is a generous giver who neither refuses nor reproaches anyone" (1:5).

Early in my life, Fred, I became aware that God would have some in every congregation who would possess this gift in all its fullness. These holy members of the body have blessed my life as I have served as their pastor. They have met with me at 5:30 in the morning for prayer meetings, when the needs of the body could be freely mentioned during intercession. They have talked with me in the privacy of a moving car about serious moral defaults in the lives of brothers and sisters, and have helped me find the mind of God for dealing with those problems. These dear ones have, on occasion, felt free to come to me in the spirit of Christ, suggesting "blind spots" in my ministry. I have never rejected their counsel in such a time, for it was always obvious that the Spirit was flowing through them. Their insight into ways to apply the Word to life situations has been invaluable.

For me, they usually have been men. Occasionally, they have been women: one was in her late seventies, and carried my confidences and her counsel unspoken to the grave.

Believing that the manner in which West Memorial deacons elected their chairman proved he was *God's* man, for many months I met regularly—usually for a weekly lunch date—with this man (whoever he was) to "brief" him on my problems.

Never—*not one time*—in my quarter century of trusting, has there ever been a betrayal of confidence. Those who possess this gift of wisdom, by the very nature of it, may always be trusted to hold confidences.

In the second chapter of 1 Corinthians a lengthy passage expounds the qualities of this gift of wisdom. Paul explains that he shared with that body without using subtle arguments, "so that your faith might be built not upon human wisdom but upon the power of God."

He then begins a section (v. 6-12) that qualifies the use of the gift of wisdom. He mentions that some members of the body are not "ripe for it." Perhaps the first example of the gift is in knowing when *not* to use it. Those who are carnal do not even possess the capacity to *hear* words of wisdom: "Few of you are men of wisdom, by any human standard" (1:26). Spiritual maturity is necessary to receive the Spirit's counsel from a fellow member of the body.

This quality, too, will be noted in those having the gift. Often they will permit the Spirit to keep them silent when others might speak out. One godly saint used to say about members of the body who were out of fellowship. "Leave them to Papa. He does not need our help. He will deal with them more wisely than we could. Keep silent." He knew that all the exhortation, advice, or counsel could not accomplish as much as "Papa" could do.

The Corinthian church was full of immature babies in Christ. They were filled with jealousy, strife, living in their lower nature. Sexual immorality was rampant. Self-satisfaction and doctrinal error of the grossest sort marked this pitiful body.

Little wonder that Paul only referred in passing (1:7) to the great wisdom God had given him to share with the churches. Such an experience-oriented congregation would have distorted the amazing wisdom which Paul revealed in depth to the more mature Colossian body (Col. 1:24-27).

Carnality within the church as a way of life, then, can smother the use of this gift. For it to be freely utilized, the body must have advanced toward maturity.

How does *the gift of putting the deepest knowledge into words* differ with the gift of wisdom? The gift of wisdom involves *insight* into the application of the deepest knowledge. It goes a step beyond it. The gift of knowledge involves an ability to gather all the facts together as the Spirit reveals them, and to communicate them. The gift of wisdom applies those facts to practical situations. Often one who can do the latter must depend on another member of the body for the knowledge.

The gift of putting the deepest knowledge into words is given to the scholars of the kingdom. We need such men in the church today. They are placed in the body because they delight in lengthy study.

Perhaps this analogy breaks down too easily, but the comparison can be made between the physicians who spend a lifetime in a laboratory doing research, and the general practitioners in the greater community. The G.P. must depend upon the researcher; often the researcher lacks the capacity to apply his findings to life situations.

I recently ran across a case in point. In a Houston medical school recently, a young doctor-to-be was accepted *only* after he signed a statement promising that he would never practice medicine beyond the point of research. He was so poorly suited to deal with the people that the examiners felt they would do him a disservice by encouraging him in that direction. However, his faculties were so perfectly prepared for research that they felt he could make gigantic contributions to the advancement of medicine.

Such a distinction can be made between these two "spirituals."

Men equipped for putting knowledge into words are needed in many places in the Lord's work. They are required to translate the Scriptures into the hundreds of languages in the world where a Bible still does not exist. Such men may not possess the gift of prophecy, but they pave the way for those who do. Our family visited the Kechi Indians of Guatemala recently, and saw our fine Southern Baptist missionaries building on the foundation of earlier missionaries who had lived among the Kechis long enough to put their language into a written form and translate the Bible for them. The churches now exploding in that tribe are filled with the power of God! Hundreds are being harvested in a true "people movement." Those with the gift of knowledge paid a lonely price, but the results will be eternally glorious!

Such study and communication is the work of the Holy Spirit in the life of the believer. It is not the fruit of the natural intelligence, but rather the result of a mature walk with God through the pages of Scripture.

How does the present church structure the use of this gift? Is it recognized and respected? Is there any situation other than the teaching of a Sunday School class where it can be used to the profit of the body?

Is there another William Carey waiting to be set free in our midst?

Carey had an insatiable appetite for study. Converted at seventeen, he joined the Congregational church. He taught himself how to read the Greek New Testament. He became a Baptist by its study and was immersed on October 5, 1783. Serving as a lay pastor, he supported himself by cobbling shoes. On the bench before him was his Greek Testament, and on the wall beside him a map of India. He added Hebrew, Latin, French, and Dutch to his languages.

His gift of putting the deepest knowledge into words was destined to be used in India. The call of the Holy Spirit to his heart was unmistakable. Unfortunately, the structures of the Baptist denomination in his day did not include a regard for the sharing of the gospel with the heathen. Leaders ignored the shoe cobbler in the body, and refused to accept his gift and his calling as valid.

Finally, the man with the gift of knowledge put it into words for a cynical clergy, and they acquiesced to his teaching that "no man deserves to hear the gospel twice until all men have had a chance to hear it once." He broke out of their shackled minds. In Kettering, England, he organized the first modern missionary society.

His forty years in India never included a single furlough. Although he had received other significant gifts from the Spirit, his gift of knowledge was always recognized as the supreme one in his life. Because of it, he mastered numerous dialects, established churches, and became a professor of Bengali and Sanskrit at Fort William College in Calcutta. The record of his accomplishments is staggering. He published the first newspaper in India. He translated the first Bible. He superintended the translation of the Bible into 42 separate Oriental languages, and as a result brought the Scriptures to a third of the people of the earth! He also wrote grammars and dictionaries for six major Indian languages, and established Serampore College. He caused laws to be passed outlawing the sacrifice of children to heathen deities. He stopped the horrible practice of burning widows alive on the funeral pyres of their dead husbands.

He has been referred to as "the greatest and most versatile Christian missionary sent out in modern times." Until his death on June 9, 1834, he faithfully followed the leadership of his Head, from whom his holy gift flowed. His theme should be passed on to each member of the body who is the recipient of that same "spiritual" . . . "EXPECT GREAT THINGS FROM GOD; ATTEMPT GREAT THINGS FOR GOD."

Fred, somehow we've got to figure out a way to respect

and properly use this gift when found among the members of the body, other than by packing the gifted one off to teach at a seminary! One refreshing possibility for us to consider is taking place right now in Indonesia. There, the missionaries voted to formally close the seminary, which had limited its scope to the training of a few men bound for the pastorate. The faculty was scattered abroad among the churches. In essence, what had occurred had to do with the releasing of the captivity of the gift of knowledge. It was injected into the mainstream of the laity. They were encouraged to recognize that *all* Christians are ministers, and all gifts are to be exercised. Schools were set up in various communities, and seminary professors taught laymen. House churches were encouraged, and laymen began to lead them in prophesying and teaching!

Back at the beginning of our journey together, you had wondered what would happen if a *real* revival came to your church. When the moving of the Holy Spirit brought *real revival to Indonesia*, the gift of knowledge was circulated freely among the body. Makes lots of sense, when you think about it! Emotional bubble baths burst quickly. A genuine Spirit-given revival will not be marked by emotionalism, but by putting deep knowledge into words. After all, the major task of the Spirit is to teach the truths about Christ.

Would he not have infinitely more impact through expanding the use of one gift like this one, than by raising a hundred bodies from the dead? Americans have recently been disillusioned to discover that the alleged "miracles" reported in the Indonesian revival have ranged from pure hoaxes to vivid expansions of the truth. What we have *not* gotten excited over, *and we should have*, was the closing of a seminary to prepare the laity for ministry! Some day we'll rejoice at the harvest of souls which will be the inevitable result of this action.

5. The Paraclete Gift

The final verbal gift is referred to in Romans 12:8 as the "gift of stirring speech." Again, the Greek word gives fathoms of meaning to this simple description. It is from the same word family that is used to describe the Holy Spirit as our Comforter in John 14, 15, and 16. There he is portrayed as "One who is called alongside to help us." By studying his role as our Paraclete, we develop a broader understanding of the paraclete gift and its function.

The Comforter is one who understands our deepest agonies, and can be expected to interpret them to the Father when all we are able to do is groan in anguish. In the same way, one with this gift has the spiritual capacity to *empathize*; that is, to suffer along with another, and to lift that one in prayer.

The Comforter is one who speaks on our behalf. He is described in the paraclete sense as being a lawyer, who guides us by his expertise in the midst of a trial. Even so, the member of the body who receives this gift may find himself aiding another by reconciling, pleading, or defending for that person.

The Comforter is further described as one who will guide us into all truth. He will take others by the hand and introduce them to Christ and his teachings. Possessors of the paraclete gift will be capable of providing the word of truth to those being assisted.

Fred, do you get the idea that this kind of "speech" is soft, confidential, and punctuated by long periods of careful listening to the other person? You are right! This "spiritual" requires the deepest levels of sensitivity to the needs of others and a compassion to help. It involves *wisdom, knowledge, helps, discerning of spirits*, and other gifts as collaterals. It will not function alone, but in connection with other grace gifts.

As Dr. Earl Rademacher says, this person encourages others by saying, "Cheer up! Our God is *omnicompetent*!" There is a divine strength imparted by the user of this gift to those who are broken in spirit. This "spiritual" is required in the body to bind up the wounded ones and to deal with the crisis situations.

We have a modern word to describe one who has this gift: *counselor*. The faster the world changes, the greater will be the need for this *paraclete* "spiritual" within the body.

76

Speed seems to make all human relationships vibrate!

This gift is extremely valuable in our outreach to the "unchurchables." It is one of the keys to an effective TOUCH ministry.

"TOUCH" stands for *Transforming Others Under Christ's Hand*. Scores of churches in the United States, Europe, and Commonwealth nations have now accepted the word, and the concept of ministry which accompanies it, from Houston's West Memorial Baptist Church. "The People Who Care" have no intention of copyrighting it . . . it's a gift of love to the family!

Our body's paraclete gift is applied to ministering to unbelievers. We use the word "outsider" to describe the *unchurchable* unbelievers. They are the specific group usually ignored by the body. But they represent up to 61 percent of each community!

Five years ago, we recognized that they would not be caught dead in their own coffins in a church building. So for four years we didn't have one. When we finally built, we built, we built a 17,000-square-foot structure that looks like anything *but* a church. It can care for about 900 for worship, over 800 for Sunday School, but in a matter of minutes it can be converted into a skating rink, coffee house, gymnasium, center for therapy, dialogue, and a *jillion other things*. We do not even use the *word* "church" to refer to it. *We* are the church. *It* is the "TOUCH CENTER." It's busy practically all day long, every day!

Most of the time, those who come to Touch Center are unchurchables who have no intention of worshipping with us. We meet them playing football, bumper pool, or volleyball. Women come for Wednesday exercise classes and stay for Bible study. Buddhists from Japan come to learn English and meet Jesus. The list of ministries goes on and on . . . .

The paraclete gift is absolutely essential to these ministries. Every one of our members in TOUCH is one "called alongside to help" someone in some way. Openness and honest sharing must mark the use of this gift in a TOUCH ministry. Loving sinners—while hating the sin in their lives—is mandatory!

. . . And right *here* is where I want to add another characteristic to the others listed. . . .

The Paraclete is called alongside to convict of sin, righteousness, and judgment to come. One who exercises this gift will not sidestep the important issue of calling sin . . . SIN. Over-permissive sympathy for sinful living is not a part of the work of the Holy Spirit! Authentic Christian love is "touch love." It's the kind that says, "I care too much about you to wink at what will bring you face-to-face with the judgment for your sin. I love you deeply, and I can no more condone your rebellious living than I could be unconcerned if you had terminal cancer. I hate *anything* which could destroy you . . . and sin is the worst destroyer known to man."

It is *this* aspect of the paraclete gift that some translators have in mind when they use words like "stirring speech" or "exhorting" to define it. But it involves infinitely more than these words. That's why the simple term "paraclete gift" appeals to many Bible students.

Of course, we would expect this gift to be coupled closely with the nonverbal gift of helps, or showing mercy. One involves *acts* of love, while the other requires *words* of love. The two are almost inseparable.

It's my conviction that all maturing believers will discover this gift within their new nature. It is used in sharing Christ with unbelievers, caring for new converts, visiting the sick, helping those in personal and family crises, and consoling the grieving.

This being the case, the equipping pastor will seek to give assistance to the development of this gift among the members of the body. For example, our deacons at West Memorial have no executive powers whatsoever. They are ministers to the flock. Each one is assigned six to eight families, and they pastor them. This paraclete gift is extremely important to their work.

Those who serve in TOUCH ministries are given 13 hours of training, and a great deal of it has to do with the ministry of counseling. This training course is now written as a book,

The Touch of the Spirit (Broadman, 1972). A 48-page workbook is also used by the local congregation. The instruction is now completely in the hands of the laity, as is the supervision of TOUCH ministries.

By bringing each new member of the body through TOUCH Basic Training, the gift is "stirred up within" those who have it. No pressure is put upon those who finish the training. Some are too immature to begin a ministry just then. Others may not have the required gifts for certain ministries. As the Holy Spirit calls forth the use of the gifts, new TOUCH ministries are born. The important thing is that the new member has been taught to observe the things the Head has commanded. Emphasis is on the *being*; the *doing* is a natural, unpressured result.

Fred, when the gift of the paraclete is functioning among the body members, the pastoral role also demands an unusual expression of that gift. Dozens of contacts with "outsiders" each week means a continual uncovering of deep problems in families, marriages, and young people. Those beyond the scope of the gifts and experience of the members find their way to the pastor. In the past several years, so many of these hurting people have come for counseling that I could easily have put my full time into doing it. My constant referrals to a Spirit-filled, practicing psychiatrist in our body has helped with a part of the load.

Another part has been lightened by means of small groups of problemed persons who interact. In these groups, the *greatest* spiritual assistance is given by body members who participate regularly. On Monday and Tuesday nights my wife Ruth and I meet with divorcees. Some in each group are committed Christians who have the gift of the paraclete. We do little more than guide the discussion. The *real* ministry comes when one of our gals responds to a tragic story told by an outsider with comments like, "Mary, I know exactly how you feel. I have been through every one of the situations you have described tonight to us. Let me tell you about it . . . "

Silently I have watched the eyes of the outsider as one who has found victory through Christ in her identical circumstance tells her brutally frank story. I have seen those eyes brim full of longing for Christ. I have seen members of the body minister on the basis of their own hurts in ways impossible for a professionally trained counsellor. I have prayed silently over and over again, "Thank you, Lord, for your "spirituals" given to our body."

Fred, look over your list of offices to be filled by the nominating committee. Got any which permit this gift of the paraclete to be used? If the Spirit is in the body, he will use all eleven of these gifts for the glory and honor of the Head. We must prayerfully search our hearts for any limits we place on him. One of those unnecessary limitations may simply be the unawareness of how these gifts are to be manifested. Building baskets to hold them is better than boxes to keep them out. By "boxes" I refer, of course, to tradition-bound systems of structuring ministries. Change is never easy; it's always necessary!

8
From the Well, a Stream . . .

"Whoever drinks the water that I shall give him will never suffer thirst any more. The water that I shall give him will be an inner spring always welling up for eternal life" (John 4:14).

"If anyone is thirsty let him come to me; whoever believes in me, let him drink. As Scripture says, 'Streams of living water shall flow out from within him.' He was speaking of the Spirit which believers in him would receive later" (John 7:37-39).

Fred, the knowledge of these eleven "spirituals" has whetted your appetite for further discussion about how one *discovers* his gifts, hasn't it? Well, let's get down to business and talk that through.

First of all, I can tell you that the gifts we saw in the bottom of the well aren't doing anyone much good. Have you ever walked past a fountain, perhaps in a fancy restaurant, and noticed all the money in the bottom of it? They usually call it a "wishing well," don't they?

In talking with Christians, I often get the idea they have a "wishing well" complex concerning the gifts. They wish they knew what they were, or how to use them.

I recall an embarrassing moment some years ago when one of my preschool sons was found on his stomach, scooping the coins out of a very shallow wishing well in a shopping center. The money in that well was designated for a home for crippled children, and the manager of the mall rightly felt indignant that my kid was helping himself. As we walked away from my place of profuse apologies, my little guy said, "Dad, they aren't gonna help many crippled children by letting all that money soak in that water! That's stupid!"

He had enough sense to know that coins are of no value in a fountain. Not until they are removed and used are they precious.

In Tokyo a couple of years ago I looked out the window of a jet inbound from Taiwan. As we hurtled across the ground to a stop, I saw men climbing around on a whole fleet of jumbo jets. Any one of them could have transported 350 passengers to the States in a matter of hours.

A half month later, I flew onto that same runway, and there sat the same ten jumbos! They had not moved a foot in all that time. A multimillion dollar investment sat unused, unflown, *because of a strike*! They could just as well have been sculptured out of wet clay by a Japanese artist, rather than to have been manufactured from some of the rarest metals in the earth.

Because of human problems, they could not fly!

The same reason causes latent spiritual gifts to remain in the well. Some of those human problems include . . . .

1. *Disobedience to God's commands.* Too many in the body are so involved in building homes and businesses, getting educated or enjoying hobbies, to *care* whether they have any coins in the well! There must be a dying to the self-life before gifts will be discovered.

Amy Carmichael disturbed others by her simple statement that when she went to India she simply "put away" the desires for earthly things. Her life and her pen have verified the reality of her statement. There must be a continuing process in the life of the Christian, which begins by an act of turning to the Head in full submission: "Leaving your former way of life, you must lay aside that old human nature which, deluded by its lusts, is sinking towards death" (Eph. 4:22).

This verse is followed by a description of what God does in response. *Acting upon* us in response to our obedience, the Spirit makes us new in mind and spirit. The new nature of *God's* creating will then show itself "in the just and devout life called for by the truth." The items to be thrown off are listed by Paul: falsehood; anger; stealing; cursing; grieving the Spirit; spite; passion; angry shouting; bad feelings; fornication; indecency of any kind; ruthless greed; coarse, stupid, or flippant talk. He summarizes with, "Make sure what would have the Lord's approval."

2. *Unwillingness to be used.* A few years ago my heart was broken by a woman who said very frankly to me that her home and her children were important to her. She had no intention of risking them to become totally committed to Christ! Seldom has anyone been that frank with me about this matter, but it obviously is the attitude of a large number of Christians today. I have watched her over the years. She has a "bamboo curtain" around the territorial limits prescribed by her for the Holy Spirit. She has already decided exactly how many hours of her week she will share with the Lord; when that maximum is reached, down comes the curtain. Heartbreaking!

Scripture teaches us that, in his own time, "Papa" will deal with her rebellion. He will shape her into the image of Christ, and needs no assistance from me to do it. But, oh! What that shaping will cost her in pain and suffering! How unnecessary it all would be, if her heart were only soft and pliable to his touch. Tragic to the life of the body is this useless limb, hanging as a dead burden to be dragged around by the other members. Coins in the fountain, unspent and unblessing, wasted! What will she say about the talent she buried in the ground when she comes to her day of judgment before God?

How in contrast to her was a beautiful young wife who struggled with this issue in Chateau d'Oex, Switzerland, recently. Following my morning message, she went to her hotel room sobbing. Through her husband, she sent word for me to come at once. I found her sitting on the floor in deepest anguish. She said, "Ralph, I have three idols in my heart. One of them is Bill. The other two are my children. I have said again and again, 'God, you can have anything in my life but those three people. Don't touch them!' But I know I must bury them. They must not live in my heart. It belongs only to my Lord. But it's a big job to have to do by myself. I need your help. Will you conduct their funeral service with me?"

Like Abraham, she placed her loved ones on the altar, willing to see the blade of the knife go through their hearts. God *must* have first place! By name, she removed them as idols to be worshiped. First, the children, one by one. Then, with great groans of surrender, we buried her precious-as-life-itself Bill!

When it was over, she stood to her feet with a heavenly glow upon her face. That glow has remained for months. And, surprise! Her husband and children are blessed with good health! God is a good God . . . he does not reward his obedient children with the destruction of their loved ones, simply because they have been sacrificed to him.

From the well, a stream . . . and in that stream she has found spiritual gifts.

Fred, I could go on and on with this list, but your own dear pastor constantly helps you conduct further self-examination of this sort. You probably have already developed a list of three or four more that you would like to add. Let me move on to another point I want to make:

"SPIRITUALS" ARE DISCOVERED IN THE *STREAM*, NOT THE *WELL*.

It's like the old prospector who would take his mule up into the Colorado mountains. To find gold, he would sift in the streams. The nuggets in the stream told him gold was around. It's the same with finding our gifts. The important thing is to *get into the flowing*. Christians who stand around waiting for the gifts to appear before they begin to minister never do anything at all!

You see, some gifts must be put into operation in order that other gifts may be developed. The more mature gifts will not be bestowed until spiritual growth has taken place. Take the gift of prophecy, for example. That will be found in the stream many miles away from some of the earlier gifts, like the gift of helps or the gift of giving.

Philip is a perfect example of what I'm talking about. He first appears in connection with a bunch of griping Grecian widows. It seems they had decided that Jewish prejudice among the apostles was keeping them from getting their fair share of the daily distribution of food. The Apostles decided they would put some men with Grecian backgrounds on a special committee, and let them worry about the problem. (All seven of the names listed in Acts 6 are Grecian!)

I can imagine the scene: Peter sidles up to Philip, and says, "Those poor widows have nothing to do during the daytime hours. They sit and brood among themselves. They complain and make trouble. We have an *exciting job* for you, Phil! Will you help them? We have discerned that you are a Spirit-ful man. You walk with God, and your gifts include wisdom. Will you take the job?"

One gift has been recognized in Philip at this point: the "spiritual" of wisdom. Philip had been in the Scriptures. He had been in the prayer closet. He had learned the ways of God.

The recognition of that gift had flowed from his life as he had quietly spoken—and not spoken—with wisdom. It qualified him for the job. Now, his appointment by the twelve called forth from him another gift: the gift of *helps*. That gift is marked by availability. Philip was available! He accepted the job.

It really wasn't the kind of job that got mentioned much from the platform. It required a lot of patient reasoning with neurotic women. The pay was terrible! But Philip flowed with the life of the Spirit, and the problems involved were solved.

What would have happened in Philip's life if he had said, "Well, Peter, I really don't know that I am cut out for that job. It may demand a great deal of time, and we are just getting ready for inventory at the plant. That's probably going to tie me up for three days, and . . . uh . . ."

I believe I know *exactly* what would have happened to

him! It would be what has happened to scores of Christians I have pastored through the years who have said things like that to the Lord. The Holy Spirit sits down outside their front door and says, *"I'm not coming into your house until you become available."*

We would have not read another thing about Philip in Acts if he had refused. But . . . *he said YES to Peter!* And so we see the well flowing as all artesian wells do, and a river of living water comes pouring out. That's really what the "spirituals" are all about: ways by which the indwelling Spirit can flow through us to the needs of the body.

To the gift of wisdom—developed by study and prayer—now add the gifts of helps, giving, paraclete, and . . . Fred, *you* ought to be able to assemble that list yourself! They were discovered in the stream of ministry, not the well.

Next, Philip is found in Acts 8:5 over in Sebaste, a huge center of population in Samaria. He is now exercising the gifts of prophecy and the discerning of spirits. The Holy Spirit found a man he could trust! From the experiences with Grecian widows, he has matured into the exercising of more responsible gifts. In Acts 8:35, the same obedient man is discovered exercising the gift of teaching. Finally settling down in Caesarea (compare 8:40 with 21:8), a city by the sea, he stayed put for twenty years, serving with his gifts. Paul made it a point to call on him when passing through on the way to Jerusalem. Already his four daughters, unmarried, had grown to such spiritual maturity that they exercised the gift of prophecy: a great tribute to their father's life.

Romans 15:13 is such a beautiful verse in relation to this thought: "And may the God of hope . . . THE SOURCE

    fill you . . . HIS SERVICE

with all joy and peace . . . OUR SATISFACTION

 by your faith in him . . . THE STIPULATION

until, by the power of the Holy Spirit . . . THE STRENGTH

you overflow with hope . . . THE STREAM!

Regardless of the age of the new convert, there are gifts which can be put to use at once by him. The Holy Spirit wishes to flow from every life. He wants every member of the body to be involved in its function. He will not wait for great levels of maturity to develop before flowing.

Any baby Christian will be able to flow with the gift of helps and giving, to begin with. The teaching of the new convert should focus around the knowledge of these truths. Their motto might well be:

FOR GROWING,
GET FLOWING!

9

"Throw It on the Wall, and See if It Sticks!"

"Do not neglect the spiritual endowment you possess, which was given you, under the guidance of prophecy, through the laying on of the hands of the elders as a body" (1 Tim. 4:14).

"That is why I now remind you to stir into flame the gift of God which is within you through the laying on of my hands" (2 Tim. 1:6).

In addition to letting the well flow as a stream, the discovery of the "spirituals" requires submission to the body. One truly authentic way to find your spiritual gifts, Fred, is by checking things out with the brothers and sisters in the family. It's important to be able to say to the group, "What do you think my gifts are?" From the beginning of the church, some of the "spirituals" have been discovered only through being in proper fellowship with the body.

A little-known detail in the life of the great Dr. George W. Truett illustrates this perfectly. Converted at age 19, he followed his parents from Georgia to Whitewright, Texas. At age 23, he attended the formal business meeting of his church, the Whitewright Baptist Church. After a season of prayer, the various members of the congregation stood to their feet to share a common insight given them concerning young Truett. One man said, "The Lord has given me a burden for George. I must share with you my conviction that he is being called to preach." Others acknowledged that, during the season of prayer, the Lord had affirmed the same truth in their hearts. All eyes turned to the young man in question.

. . . Can you imagine that happening in your church this Saturday afternoon? What would be the reaction of a typical young person age 23, to such a statement today? Back in 1890 . . .

George W. Truett stood to his feet, deeply moved. He confessed he had felt no such call of God in his own heart. He also indicated that he considered it mandatory to be obedient to what God was calling him to do through the word given to the body.

That night, George W. Truett was ordained as a preacher of the gospel!

Not a soul on the face of the globe can contest the reality of that call. From September, 1897 until July, 1944—the date of his death—he served as the pastor of the First Baptist Church of Dallas. His influence stretched across the continent, and then the world, in witness for Jesus Christ. Few men of his generation were as powerful in the pulpit.

Two things about that occasion haunt me:

1. The sensitivity to the Spirit by the members of the congregation. They were closely related to each other, and assumed a posture of body life which made such a call possible.

2. The sensitivity of one member of that body to the work of the Spirit within it. The immediate response Truett gave required a deep level of trust to have been shaped in him well in advance of that Saturday afternoon.

It is a direct repetition of the ordination of Paul and Barnabas, mentioned earlier. The Greek text in Acts 13:1-2 does not limit the prayer meeting to the five names mentioned. Rather, they were simply included among those in the congregation at the time the Spirit set the two men apart. It was a body meeting, and the call was to the body to release two of their number for the work of the Lord.

The discovery of spiritual gifts will require such a relationship. Blessed is the church in which it exists! Let me tell you about the way God made all of this very real and practical for the family at West Memorial . . .

Stiles came to our fellowship for a number of weeks before the Lord directed the Spirit to connect him to us. In the weeks that followed, he was elected by the body to serve as a deacon. He and Diane faced the call of the body for this service with much prayer. Pastoring six families of the congregation is a full-time job! God rewarded him for his obedience with the development of latent "spirituals," and I began to get feedback from his families. His gifts of verbal and non-verbal manifestations had endeared him to his little flock.

The Spirit then began to call forth a 33-year-old insurance executive to serve in the office of a pastor. He said to me one Sunday, "Ralph, I'm struggling with a deep problem! I must see you."

One afternoon later, he explained that he felt he ought to sell his house, pay off the small debts he owed, and go to seminary. Later in the week, Diane joined us for a time of sharing about his call. The *Big Question* for Stiles was also bothering his wife. She said, "I am ready to follow Stiles to the end of the earth, ready to go anywhere and do anything. But I do not know at this point whether he has the gifts of prophecy and teaching, and they are essential to the office of a pastor. I must be sure about this before I will feel right about selling out and going to seminary."

She was so right! Seminaries are not designed to produce spiritual gifts in a man: they can only sharpen what is already present. You can't sharpen a knife if there is no blade. The thing we needed to discover was, does Stiles have these latent gifts? I suggested that the body needed to tell us the answer to that question. I would arrange preaching and teaching situations for him, and he would not discuss the matter further with anyone. If the body recognized the presence of the gifts, we would take this as the word from the Lord.

At this time, Stiles' sense of humor brimmed over. He said, "One time I heard about a young girl who married into an Italian family. She so wanted to please her new husband with her cooking, but he kept telling her she did not cook the spaghetti until it was done. Finally, she went to her mother-in-law, and asked her what to do. Looking around to be sure the men were not listening, the mother-in-law replied, 'Honey, you throw it against the wall, and see if it sticks!' Let's do that with my call to preach, Ralph. We'll throw it against the body and see if it sticks."

At that time we had a TOUCH ministry in a KOA trailer park in our community. On Saturday nights about sundown, a vesper service would be held for the vacationers there. I arranged for Stiles to preach in that setting. There, between pinball machines and a noisy air conditioner, he held forth.

Feedback came from within the body. Stiles could preach. Next, I arranged for him to preach to the congregation. More feedback: there was clear recognition of the gift of prophecy. Diane's eyes danced as she said to me, "He's got it!"

The Armageddon coffee house was in full blast that summer. A hangout for teenagers, we had various groups meeting there for fellowship, recreation, and Bible study. One night I was caught in a conflict of commitments. I called Stiles: "Friend, a pastor is supposed to be ready to serve at the drop of a hat, and be on his way before the hat hits the ground! Will you work with the teenagers tonight?" Stiles replied, "I'm on my way."

About midnight, my college-aged son came through the back door of our house saying, "Wow! We had Stiles Watson with us tonight at Armageddon. Dad, you should have heard him teach. He really got to us. In fact, the meeting just broke up. Not only did he share deep things from the Word, but he was so concerned about the kids who came that he seemed to just reach out and draw them into the truths he was presenting. He really ought to be doing more teaching with our teenagers."

As my son, a member of the body said "Goodnight" and headed towards his bedroom, I bowed my head, and said, "Thank you, Lord, for the word from the body!" I went to the telephone and dialed Stiles' number. He had just walked in the door, and answered it as it rang for the first time:

"Stiles, you had better call the realtor first thing in the morning," I said. "The spaghetti has stuck all over the wall!"

I watched that dear couple as they sold out everything they had accumulated for a lifetime, and headed for the seminary. Then came lean months, with practically no income. A church did not open up. With five mouths to feed, Stiles took a job requiring him to walk around the seminary campus as a night watchman. He shared with me his loneliness during those nights, and the new levels of faith God had taught him and Diane through it all. Ruth and I dispatched a monthly check to him, and I prayed daily for him.

Then, after many months, an excited telephone call came from him. The First Baptist Church of Joy, Texas, had called him to be their pastor! As he shared his excitement with me, I realized that the validation of his gifts by our body had been necessary to keep him going during the desert season.

I told him it looked like the spaghetti was still stuck on the wall!

Just about five months ago Stiles came back to the People Who Care, to become the third man in four years to be ordained by the body. As our deacons came, one by one, to lay their hands upon his head in setting him apart for the defense of the gospel, I was moved to tears. Diane was kneeling by his side, ready to go to the ends of the earth with him.

His submission to the body life was symbolized by his kneeling form. His obedience to the Spirit was symbolized by his bowed head.

Guess that's the first piece of spaghetti I ever saw in a blue serge suit!

Fred, there is a great relationship available within the body life when we accept the responsibility for helping the other members discover their gifts. The point Paul was making in the eleventh chapter of 1 Corinthians was necessary because that carnal congregation did not care about each other. They ate together, but would not share their food with each other. They joined in a common cup of wine in observing the Lord's Supper, but they did not have a common respect for the others in the body life. They fell into sharply divided groups. Paul warned that they were in danger of judgment when they partook of an ordinance which is meant to be a group action, and did it as unrelated individuals. The body of Christ is the body of my brother and my sister. I honor Christ when I honor them, and I disgrace Christ when I do not assume a personal responsibility and concern for them. He says, "For he who eats and drinks eats and drinks judgment on himself if he does not *discern the body*. That is why many of you are feeble and sick, and a number have died" (11:29-30).

Body members should be alert to the spiritual needs and strengths of the others in the congregation. For this to occur, there must be a system of fellowship which permits intimate relations to develop. This cannot take place when our only contact with each other is in a one-hour Sunday School class and a depersonalized worship service. Even committee meetings often are too hurried and structured to allow much of an interchange to occur among members. The *agape* (love) feasts of the early church afforded this free time for fellowship.

There are many ways of solving this problem in the contemporary church. Keep in mind that the Jerusalem church had many thousands of members, and they were not too large to have this *koinonia*, or *fellowship*.

At West Memorial, we have tried to solve the problem in the manner by which the deacons work with their families. Gatherings in homes of the deacon families occur frequently. I have encouraged these groups to be totally unstructured—no games or outside speakers! The need is for time to sit and talk.

TOUCH Ranch is the big solution for us! Located in the rolling bluebonnet countryside only one hour from our homes, this 117-acre farm actually belongs to one of our member families. They have donated over 40 acres of it as a future site for our own retreat facility. For five years, we have gone to live together there for weekends. Thirty to fifty people pile into the farmhouse, bunkhouse, barn, and now a

65-foot-long trailer donated to the ranch by one of the members. The deacons are in charge of these retreats, which begin Friday night and continue until Sunday night. Those who are on retreat are not expected to be back for Sunday services at TOUCH Center. They conduct their own worship service, where even children are encouraged to share and sing for the others.

We have gradually developed a life-style for our retreats. Outside speakers have been used, but we usually lose something when they come in without knowing us intimately. We usually limit the group to our own body.

Doing our own cooking permits the women to get to know each other. Work projects permit the men to get a feel for how hard the other fellow digs in. Taking the kids along shows up true temperaments (and tempers!) by Saturday night. We try to keep about 75 percent of the hours totally unstructured, with just enough group discussion to give everyone a chance to "pipe up" with their convictions and opinions about things. We accept the fact that growth, whether spiritual, emotional, intellectual, or physical, requires a certain amount of tension. As long as there is not personal hostility involved, we encourage honesty rather than politeness in these "rap sessions."

Other than these brief structured periods, the group is free to sleep, read, watch television, play games, hike, be together with the kids, or send the kids back to the huge tree that is perfect for climbing, and contains three treehouses.

Not long ago, Ruth and I spent two days at TOUCH Ranch alone. As I sat on the side porch for an hour I recalled the many lives we have truly touched to the depths in the retreats. I pictured again in my mind's eye a pastor who brought six or eight of his members to the ranch, and asked me to be their convenor. On a Saturday afternoon, that group melted into each other in a way that saved a church from serious division. The lovely old rug we sat on for that session was filled with wet spots from tears when the sharing time was over.

The Whitewright Baptist Church of 1890 did not need

such innovations as retreat sites. They *were* a retreat site! Isolated, without electricity, subject to fierce storms, those people were forced to rely upon each other. In that context, levels-of respect developed. From those levels of respect, trust was born. From that trust, George Truett didn't bat an eye when the group informed him he was going to be a preacher.

I submit that we *need* to provide this kind of a relationship for every single congregation today if we are to be in a position to call forth gifts within the body's members.

Throw it against the wall, and see if it sticks!

10
Gifts Lead to Ministries

"Whatever gift each of you may have received, use it in service to one another, like good stewards dispensing the grace of God in its varied forms. Are you a speaker? Speak as if you uttered oracles of God. Do you give service? Give it as in the strength which God supplies. In all things so act that the glory may be God's through Jesus Christ; to him belong glory and power for ever and ever. Amen" (1 Pet. 4:10-11).

In 1 Corinthians 12:4-6 there are three divisions made by Paul concerning the "spirituals." Thus far we have discussed only the first of those divisions: the varieties of gifts. The second division is described in these words: "There are varieties of service, but the same Lord." The gifts in verse 4 are connected to the Holy Spirit. The varieties of service are connected to the Head of the body. The Spirit manifests himself through equipping us with spiritual abilities, but it is the Lord who appoints us to our service.

Fred, this is a good place in our journey to bring up the content of the third division, so we may contrast it with the second. A bit later we'll look at it in detail. Verse six says, "There are many forms of *work*, but all of them, in all men, are the work of the same God." Note that the *Spirit* is expressly the source of the *gifts*; the *Lord* is specifically the source of our calling to specific *service*; and then *God* is mentioned as the source of *"forms of work."* The distinction made between *service* and *work* helps us to understand this passage.

The Greek word for *service* is one we have moved over into our language untranslated: *deacon*! It speaks of servant-hood, of ministering to others. It fits in perfectly with the service rendered by the eleven gifts we have studied.

Interestingly enough, the Greek word for "work" has also been moved over into our language untranslated: *energy*! This third division involves the superhuman power of God "working." It is referring to certain activities of God's energy, inserted into the stream of human activity. We shall refer to three areas as "energizings" rather than "spirituals," and deal with them later:

1. Miraculous powers
2. Gifts for judgment of the Gentiles: tongues, interpretation of tongues
3. Separate acts of restoring health to the body parts

Having made this distinction, let's give thought to the *varieties of service.* Christ the Head has designated five basic offices within the body of Christ. They are the positions of the apostles, prophets, evangelists, pastors, and teachers. In addition, other combinations of gifts will be given to each member of the body for their specific ministries.

The office of the apostle is a foundation office for the church. Once a foundation is finished, others build upon it. You do not, however, find foundations being relaid on the third or the tenth floors of a building! Even so, when the original apostles passed away, they were not replaced. Those who believe that the apostles laid hands on others and made them successors miss some important facts. The qualifications for this office are set forth in Acts 1:21-22:

1. He must have been with Jesus constantly, from the time of "John's ministry of baptism until the day when he was taken up."

2. He must have been an eyewitness to Jesus' resurrection. Paul calls himself "an apostle born out of due season," and qualifies uniquely on the basis of a heavenly vision of the

97

ascended Christ.

No others can qualify for this office, simply because the primary requirements involved a time and a place in history. In addition, Revelation 21:14 tells us, "The city wall had twelve foundation-stones, and on them were the names of the *twelve apostles* of the Lamb." Doesn't sound much like there were more apostles than that original twelve, does it, Fred?

Apostles ministered in transition days. They were given certain powers to perform "energizings" in order that they might confirm that the early church was endued with Christ's life. As that foundation fact was established, the need for the "energizings" died off. Writing about A.D. 375, the golden-tongued orator Chrysostom said, "The apostles indeed enjoyed the grace of God in abundance; but if we were bidden to raise the dead, or open the eyes of the blind, or cleanse lepers, or straighten the lame, or cast out devils and heal the like disorders," he confesses his generation to be powerless: "Of miraculous powers, not even a vestige is left."

The same word is used in a different sense by Paul on a few occasions. It literally means "sent one," and in this frame of reference an occasional reference will be made to someone who has been sent for a specific ministry to a specific place. One example of that is in Romans 16:7: "Greet Andronicus and Junias (both women's names) my fellowcountrymen and comrades in captivity. They are eminent among the *apostles* [sent ones], and they were Christians before I was."

The office of the prophet is given second place in the list of ministries in Ephesians 4:11 and also in 1 Corinthians 12:28. In both places, it is the first office to be established upon the foundation laid by the apostles. As their miraculous feats verified the presence of the Head in the church, the walls built on that foundation would be erected by preaching.

It is obvious that the office of the pastor will include this gift of prophesying, but the office of the prophet should also be filled by many members of the body. This is a difficult idea to get across to moderns, because we tend to consider "preaching" to occur only in a building on Sunday morning. If we can divorce ourselves of this concept, we can begin to see the office of the prophet as not being a threat to the office of the pastor. We should be thankful for every gift the Lord gives the body.

How many people are necessary to make up a "congregation?" During pioneer missionary days in the Northeast, I used to drive a hundred miles to preach to *three* people! At one time, we began a congregation near Rockville, Maryland, where the first congregation consisted of Ruth at the piano; me preaching, ushering, leading the singing, and collecting the offering; and *one* lady with her seven-year old daughter for the audience. Prophets don't require thousands in the audience. One is enough.

I submit that the office of a prophet should eventually include practically every member of the body! Philip practiced this office with one eunuch. Our fellowship encourages every person in the body to fill this office, and to use their own "diggings" as the scene for forth telling. The prophets can preach to the unsaved, to believers, to children, to young people, in groups or to individuals, indoors or outdoors. *This gift involves the public proclamation of the message of Christ by the body.*

Fred, 1 Corinthians 14:1 counsels *all* believers to seek to find this coin in the well. One of the first signs of maturity will be the exercising of this gift. Men and women in our body in Houston utilize this office in apartment clubhouses and rooms of their homes. All TOUCH ministries require at least one person to be present who possesses the prophetic gift and uses it. Otherwise, there would be no one to tell forth the wisdom of God revealed by the Spirit through the Word.

The office of the evangelist. In our generation, the word "evangelist" has been used to describe an itinerant preacher who specializes in sermons pointed to the nonbeliever. Such a man, however, is biblically a preacher who exercises the gift of prophecy. There is no question about the fact that some men are especially filled by the Spirit for this type of proclamation. They are endowed with the ability to touch the deepest spiritual strings of the unbeliever's heart, calling him to repentance. Perhaps one writer uses the proper term when he refers to evangelistic preaching as a *variation* of the gift of prophecy. I don't seem to have it at this stage of my flowing.

Many thousands of people across the world today can date their moment of personal commitment to services where such evangelistic preaching has occurred. Men like Dr. Billy Graham and Leighton Ford have pushed whole nations beneath the shadow of the cross with their ministries, and have authenticated for this generation the reality of mass evangelism as a means of harvesting. Without question, there will *never* be a time when a generation of men will pass by without a Wesley, Whitfield, Moody, Sunday, or Graham in its midst!

The term "evangelist" appears only three times in the New Testament. In Ephesians 4:11, it is listed immediately after the offices of the apostle and of the prophet. The second use of the word is in Acts 21:8, where Philip is described as "the evangelist." Twenty years before he had been described as settling in Caesarea, still the place of his residence when Paul passes through to briefly visit with him. How did he "evangelize"?

The final use of the word is in 2 Timothy 4:5, where the young trainee is admonished by Paul to "do the work of an evangelist." To get a full picture of the use of that word in its special use, we may learn from church historians. What *were* the acts of an evangelist?

Eusebius was a church historian who lived about A.D. 300, Fred. He has written a large and detailed history of the early church which gives us an insight into the work of evangelists at about A.D. 100: "Starting out upon long journeys they performed the office of evangelists, being filled with the desire to preach Christ to those who had not yet heard the word of faith, and to deliver to them the divine Gospels. And when they had only laid the foundations of the faith in foreign places, they appointed others as pastors, and entrusted them with the nurture of those that had recently been brought in, while they themselves went on again to

100

other countries and nations, with the grace and the cooperation of God."

Timothy was one of the first men who served as an evangelist, or *church planter*. Paul, Barnabas, Silas, Timothy, Philip . . . these are names of men who went to certain towns, and settled down to establish locally the body of Christ. They found the Lydias and baptized them. They made tents to support themselves. They developed teams of men and women who could assist them, like Priscilla and Aquila. They did not remain for a week or a month, but for perhaps two years. Philip may have started several churches near Caesarea. They did the *work of an evangelist* until a body had formed, and then they watched God call one of the body's members to become the pastor-shepherd of the flock. It was then they moved away, and they never usurped the office of that pastor by trying to take it away from him!

In Acts 8:1, the laity of the body in Jerusalem were literally "scattered like seed" over the country districts of Judea and Samaria. Caused by violent persecution in the church, it precipitated the need for the office of the evangelist to be manifested in a great way. Those evangelists were members of the laity, not apostles—and "they went through the country, preaching the word" (v. 5). It is in this context that we are introduced to Philip the *evangelist*.

Fred, the office of the evangelist is the reason hundreds of new congregations have been formed throughout the world. Sometimes these evangelists go by the name "missionaries," and they are supported by the body in the homeland. But often they are simply men and women who go to live in a new community where there is no gospel witness. They begin a work which later develops into a body with a pastor.

For some five years, I watched courageous laymen and women plant churches in New Jersey and Pennsylvania. I had the joy of serving as a "coach" to them, but they did the planting. One was an employee of a trucking firm. Another was a fine physician. Another was an FAA employee. Still another, a woman retired from military service. Altogether, I worked with twenty-eight "evangelists" in those years, and not a one of them ever asked for a thin dime of payment for their months of investment of blood, sweat, and tears!

I have only tried to set a *framework* for further Bible study about this subject for you, Fred. You will find that everything the Scripture says fits this truth. This being the case, your home church should consider every member who is transferred to a distant, unchurched community as one to be called by the Head to the office of an evangelist. When they are, for heaven's sake, *support them with your prayers and money!* Having been with them, I know what that can mean! The same goes for those who are serving as missionaries on a foreign field. Antioch Church was the sponsoring body for Paul and his associates. They prayed and supported him. As other new bodies were formed, they also sent their support . . . that's how Epaphroditus ended up in Rome. He carried support money from the Philippian church to their beloved evangelist.

The office of pastor is never mentioned in the New Testament except for one reference to it in Ephesians 4:11. Meaning "shepherd," this office is also described by the use of the words "overseer" and "elder." The qualifications and "spirituals" for this office are listed in 1 Peter 5:1-4, Titus 1: 5-9, and 1 Timothy 3:1-7.

The office of the teacher is coupled closely to that of the pastor. He must be a teacher if his flock is to grow into spiritual maturity. First Timothy 5:17 separates the gifts of preaching and teaching from leading, and indicates that the elder who can do all three is "worthy of a double stipend."

While preaching involves announcing, exhorting, and admonishing, teaching provides a total outline on a subject. It also involves dialogue with those being taught. At West Memorial, occasional Sunday evenings have been devoted to opportunities for dialogue with the pastor by the body. Answering questions from the body is one of the finest learning situations . . . for the pastor!

Happy indeed is the body who has a pastor-teacher who considers himself a "player-coach." A benevolent dictator is simply no role for a pastor; he smothers the latent gifts of the body parts. The true pastor can be encouraged to get the *ministry* of the Lord situated within the laity, where it belongs. To do this, he must not become the Hired Holy Man who serves the community on behalf of the congregation, doing all the witnessing, preaching, teaching, etc. His own attitude toward the office he holds is the best solution to a situation where others view him as a star fullback, rather than a coach.

11
The "Energizings"

"About gifts of the Spirit, there are some things of which I do not wish you to remain ignorant. You know how, in the days when you were still pagan, you were swept off to those dumb heathen gods, however you happened to be led" (1 Cor. 12:1-2).

"There are many forms of work, but all of them, in all men, are the work of the same God. In each of us the Spirit is manifested in one particular way, for some useful purpose" (1 Cor. 12:6-7).

At the beginning of the last chapter, Fred, I described the difference between the words "service" and "work" as used in 1 Corinthians 12:5-6. "Work" here can be aptly described for the modern mind as the "energizings" of God. This word in the Greek is described in Thayer's Greek-English Lexicon as being *"used only of superhuman power."* Examples which document that statement include Philippians 2:13: "For it is God who *works* in you, inspiring both the will and the *deed* [work], for his own chosen purpose." Substitute the word "energizing" in that passage, and you get an idea of its deep meaning.

In Galatians 3:5, Paul writes: "When God gives you the Spirit and *works* [energizes] miracles among you." Here the miraculous is seen to be the result of the energizing activity of God. In 2:8, God's *energizing* made Peter an apostle to the Jews and Paul an apostle to the Gentiles. Paul refers to his ministry in Colossians 1:29: "I am toiling strenuously with all the energy and power of Christ *at work* [energizing] in me." This energizing is also referred to in connection with the body life: "The whole frame grows through the due activity [energizing] of each part" (Eph. 4:16). James 5:16 tells us that the much-prevailing supplication of a righteous man *energizes* the power of God. Ephesians 3:7 tells us Paul considered his ministry to be a gift of the grace of God, according to the *energizing* of his power.

But why did Paul make a third distinction in 1 Corinthians 12:4-6? Do not all of the gifts flow from him? Are not all of them the result of his putting forth his power? Yes! According to 12:11, *all* the gifts are the result of the *energizings* of the one and the same Spirit.

Nevertheless, the Greek word for energizing carries another thought. It is connected to the visible effects caused by his holy energy. It speaks of the specific *acts* which result from his energy. The results of his activity are significantly and obviously not of man's doing in the *energizings*. Whatever those visible effects are, they will cause men to say, "*God* did that!"

Several "spirituals" not yet mentioned are of such a nature that they cause such a reaction, Fred. They are the grace of miracles, tongues, interpretations of tongues, and healings. Because of their visible effects, they have been called, "the *sign* gifts." The eleven we have already studied are called "the *service* gifts."

The eleven quietly manifest themselves in a divine flow within the body life. The four are anything but quiet! They may attract attention to themselves. When they do, they detract from the blessed Head and his Spirit. As someone has said, "To have a greater encounter with God and to come away enamored with the experience rather than with God is sophisticated adultery. We are not to magnify the gift instead of the giver. We are not to go out as an evangel for our gifts, but we are to go out as an evangel for God."

Fred, ours is a day of thrill-seekers, and of sincere people who have lived in frustration because God does not seem to exhibit himself in our society. Forgetting that the FINAL REVELATION of God was made in Jesus Christ, they seek for some new revelation which will authenticate that he is working. Scared by the radical theologians who have announced, "God is dead!" these dear ones have cried, "Give us a sign!"

Little wonder, then, that we have today a rash of fanaticism centering around the sign gifts. I am using that word "fanaticism" in the marvelous definition given it by A. J. Gordon years ago . . . "the eccentric action of doctrines that have been loosened from their connection with the Christian system."

I have little hope that what I share with you now will be of any value to those who have already been swept away by fanaticism. Many precious Christians are too caught up with the excitement of it all to earnestly think through what I am going to explain to you. Later on, there is going to be a heart-rending "fallout" from the doctrinal error now being spread. When that time comes, I want to lovingly, tenderly help those brothers and sisters back to the truth. In the meantime, I cry a lot! Let's take a careful look at what the Word teaches about the four sign gifts, in which the "energizing" is so obvious:

1. The Gift of Miracles

One definition of "miracle" is: "effects wrought immediately by God without the intervention of natural forces." Such effects occurred throughout the Old Testament. *Why?* Is there any pattern to the motive of God in performing miracles?

Yes! The God who is Spirit used this as a means of expressing himself to men. If you did not have a *body* through which you could express yourself, Fred, you would have to have some way to let others know you were present. Miracles were God's way of communicating with men. They were specifically *performed with reason:* God was saying, "You may not see me with your eye, but I AM and I am here!" I'll let you ponder the miracles of the Old Testament you can recall. They'll all fit that thought.

When our Lord came to the earth, there was a flood of miraculous activity performed by him. The Gospel of John is a life of Jesus in which specific miracles are selected and joined together. John calls them *signs*: "This deed in Cana-in-Galilee is the *first of the signs* by which Jesus *revealed his glory*." The word used here for *glory* is a word so filled with meaning that I preached for six weeks about it, Fred! In short, it is a word which refers to the total nature, or personality, of God. Get the point? The miracle of turning water into wine was the first sign that the God of Old Testament miracles was in Jesus!

The reason for God's performing miracles was the same there as it had always been. God said, "In the body of this man, I AM has come to dwell among you." Jesus' miracles were signs of his presence.

Then Jesus sent his disciples *out to proclaim that he was God*—and they were excited to discover that the Invisible One performed miracles through them. Same reason! He was saying, "I AM is in the work these men are called to do."

When the disciples saw the risen Lord ascend into the clouds, they heard him promise that his spirit would be upon them as they went to make disciples. In the months which followed, they discovered that I AM had manifested his presence among them through miracles, once again saying to those who observed the newly formed church, "I'm here!"

. . . And then, the miracles died off!

Scripture seems to indicate that the miracles did not extend beyond those believers upon whom the twelve laid hands. If we remember the purpose of the use of miracle from the very beginning, we will understand why! *Miracle* was always tied to the *revelation of God*. That revelation had been completely and finally made in the person of Jesus Christ. The entire book of Hebrews is the authentication of this. Why *should* miracles continue? I AM had come to abide within his body, the Body of Christ. With a body through which he might demonstrate his life, the miracles ceased. There was no further need to reveal himself, a Spirit, to the world. That was a finished work in Jesus Christ. Now the Holy Spirit could involve himself by the grace gifts to the body for the diffusion of the revelation to the "uttermost parts of the world."

By the end of the first century, Paul, Peter, and probably John were dead. Their students known to us from the late first and early second centuries may include Polycarp, Ignatius, Papias, and Clement. The *next* generation includes Justin and Irenaeus, who get quite vague about miracle-working. They have little exact personal acquaintance with the subject, and do not mention specific instances of miracle to which they have been eyewitnesses. John Calvin said that it was unreasonable to ask for miracles, or to expect to find them, where there is no new gospel.

THERE IS NO NEW GOSPEL! Christ has come. His work has been done. His word is complete. The "signs" that God had *energized* were no longer needed. This gift does not exist today! If it does, then we have no finished revelation. We can have one or the other. We do not have both.

Does this mean that the supernatural power of God is no longer available? Of course not! I am not saying that he does not fashion and shape bodies, circumstances, and events. Of a certainty, he does. I have a brother who is alive, who was supposed to die. A whole group of doctors told us he could not recover from being hit by a train. Upon his complete recovery, his doctor put his head in his hands and wept, confessing that only God had healed my brother.

. . . But God did not do it to prove he was still around. In that sense of the true use of the word "miracle," David's healing was *not* a miracle. It was simply the work of a loving Father who responded to the prayers of his children.

I do not believe in miracles. I believe in a finished revelation. If you have one, you can't have the other! (Now out of print, the greatest single work I have found concerning this subject is Benjamin B. Warfield's *Miracles, Yesterday and Today, Real and Counterfeit.* It was last published in 1965 by

108

Eerdmans.)

2. The Gift of Tongues

Fred, perhaps the most important single principle to keep in mind as you study the Scripture is this: *doctrine carries miracle*; miracles do not lead to doctrines. When we consider the energizing of God in the gift of tongues, we must first ask, what *doctrinal* teaching can we start out with? This is emphasized by the statement that all the gifts have "some useful purpose." What doctrinal statement explains the usefulness of this gift?

By the present practicers of it, two distinct opinions will be presented. The old-line Pentecostals feel that tongues is a way God speaks to man. Their meetings are filled with revelations from God to man, which are then interpreted. The congregation is the recipient of those words.

This, however, is clearly in violation of the *finished work of revelation* in the Scriptures. It opens a can of worms, for only personal "feeling" can judge the accuracy of such verbal revelation and its consequent interpretation. Who knows whether all this is coming from God, man, or the devil? If the Scripture is *ultimate authority*, there is simply no need for a Sunday night word from God!

The old-line Pentecostals teach holy and separated living. They preach a strong message of salvation through a personal commitment to Jesus Christ. They take a strong stand against smoking, drinking, and social excesses. They are embarrassed by their little brother!

He is the neo-Pentecostal. His ranks are filled with those who are "one in the Spirit, one in the Lord." They are, however, anything but one in doctrine! The only doctrine in common is that of the gift of tongues. They run the whole gamut of salvation doctrines, from hard-line Roman Catholic teaching through Wesleyan thought to the Reformed Covenant ideas. A bit of smoking and drinking is overlooked for the sake of "oneness."

The big embarrassment, however, lies in the fact that a *new* "useful purpose" for the tongues has been introduced.

They are no longer God's words to man. They are man's "praise languages" to God. Therefore, the Pentecostals wring their hands while the neo-Pentecostals ignore the Scriptures in 1 Corinthians 13-14 which limit the number who can so speak and also forbid more than one at a time to speak. It's an odd thing, Fred! They pick among the verses to find the ones that give them license for all to pray in tongues in unison or sing in tongues, but *skip* the restricting passages.

Another odd thing is the fact that this same phenomenon of tongues appears regularly outside the Christian faith. It has been observed in Hindu cults, African tribal groups, and even among animistic spirit-worshipers. I myself saw an exhibition of it in Haiti's remote areas, as a witch doctor finished drinking the hot blood from a decapitated rooster, and the "spirit" spoke through him.

Often I have been told that the way one can tell something is from God is by the *love* that is shown by the life of a person. "It *has* to be of God! You should have *felt* the *love* in the room!" STOP! The authority of that judgment is not from the Scripture: it's from a *feeling* . . . "You should have FELT . . ." I submit that this is one of the most dangerous possible ways to establish doctrinal truth!

A few weeks ago, a Hindu mystic who calls himself the Messiah and the son of God arrived in Houston to sit on his twenty-five-foot throne. Thousands of ex-Jesus People were among those who came from across the world to worship at his feet. I sent two of our staff members to their headquarters house in advance of the big event to scout out their teachings. The first one who reported to me said, "I'm really confused! I don't know how to judge that group. Ralph, you should have FELT THE LOVE down there. Everyone loves everyone with such sacrificial love. I thought only God's people had anything like that!"

How long will it take for us to be so shaken in this generation by the inroads of error that we will recognize that there is only ONE AUTHORITY by which we determine truth? That authority is the *Scripture*. Love is no ultimate by which truths are certified. It is the highest of all the fruits of the Spirit, but it is not our authority!

Fred, there is a clear-cut doctrinal statement in 1 Corinthians 14:20-22 that contradicts the explanations of both Pentecostal and neo-Pentecostal. Since it is the *only* doctrinal statement in the Scriptures about this matter, I must emphasize that it is, alone, of all Scripture, the authority from which *each passage* discussing the gift of tongues must be interpreted: "Do not be childish, my friends. Be as innocent of evil as babes, but at least be grown-up in your thinking. We read in the Law: 'I will speak to this nation through men of strange tongues, and by the lips of foreigners; and even so they will not heed me, says the Lord.' Clearly then these 'strange tongues' are not intended as a sign for believers, but for unbelievers."

Let's start with the quotation from the Law Paul uses. His direct quote is from Isaiah 28:11-12, where the prophet is warning unbelieving Israel that God will pronounce judgment upon them because they have refused to listen to his commands. That judgment would be rendered in the form of invading armies, who would come with "barbarous speech and strange tongue." Their foreign tongues in the midst of the holy land would, Isaiah taught, be God's voice!

Isaiah's passage can be traced to its source: Deuteronomy 28:49. There Moses is bringing his concluding charge to the nation of Israel prior to his death. Back in the fifteenth verse, a section of impending judgment begins. It is to come upon them, if they should disobey the Lord. All the verses that follow describe in Moses' prophecy what God can be expected to do to them for rejecting him. Verse 49 reads, "May the Lord raise against you a nation from afar, from the other end of the earth, who will swoop you up like a vulture, a nation whose language you will not understand." There follows a description of how this invader will tear down the walls of their cities, and leave them in starvation.

This is the Scripture Paul attaches to speaking in tongues in his time! He is disgusted that the Corinthian church played with tongues as though it were a little toy, thereby abusing it. The purpose of the energizing of the body to speak in tongues

111

was clear: it was the expression of God's judgment upon Israel for rejecting their holy Messiah. *It had a useful purpose!* God intended for the body of Christ to symbolize the coming destruction upon Israel for being disobedient. "He came unto his own, and his own received him not." From Moses and Isaiah came the pattern God would use! The symbolic meaning of the tongues was apparent to all scholars of the Old Testament. Only the "childish" would play around with such a solemn *energizing!*

Upon the understanding of this, we can interpret each one of the Acts passages where tongues occur. In each case, the coming of the Spirit into believers led them to declare judgment upon all Jews who had rejected the Messiah. Paul's irritation with the Corinthians was that they had made *other* use of this gift!

Oh, my revered Paul, what would you write if you could see what *this* generation of Corinthians has done with it? Would you approve of that meeting I attended as a spectator, where all were "getting" the gift, and where precious bodies of Christ within a three-state area who had lost their members to this quasi-church assembly WERE BEING OPENLY RIDICULED AND DERIDED? Would you have been happy about the "slaying in the Spirit" that took place, without a shred of any scriptural basis except a pitiful proof-text found in John 18:6? Would you rejoice that our precious bodies are being rendered helpless by "wolves within and without," who sap the strength and vitality of the true ministry, and teach blasphemous doctrinal errors concerning a "baptism" of the Holy Spirit which is considered as important as the new birth? How would you write were you to live in a generation when men would teach that the sole proof that you have "got the baptism" is speaking in a gibberish that computers verify has no relationship to any language known to man?

Fred, the judgment of Israel occurred in A.D. 70, exactly as Jesus had predicted in Matthew 24! A historian of that day named Josephus tells how Jews cut off parts of their bodies to curb infection, how the walls of the city and the Temple were pulled down, and how famine stalked those who held

112

out against the invading Roman army led by Titus.

. . . And then, the tongues died off!

Eusebius, quoting the earlier historian Irenaeus, includes a passage in which Irenaeus admits he has no first-hand knowledge of tongues existing in his day. Irenaeus, you recall, was in the second generation following Paul.

In 1 Corinthians 13:8-10, Paul indicates that the gifts of prophecy and putting deepest knowledge into words will continue until Christ returns. His thesis is that "the partial vanishes when wholeness comes." The verb tense is explicit in both cases. These gifts are *acted upon* at the time of their cessation; that is, they are stopped from without. Prophecy and knowledge will be gifts used until the end of this age. Then, when we are face to face with our blessed Lord, we will understand all things, and will have no need for these gifts. (Fred, as a preacher, I'm looking forward to that time: I'm going fishing for the first thousand years!)

The other gift mentioned is *tongues*. The Greek is quite significant here, for it uses a verb tense for "cease" which is in complete contrast from the one used for the other two gifts. Literally, it says "they will drop away of themselves." Like a dead leaf on a tree, which has no further useful purpose to perform!

Tongues served no useful purpose after Titus and his men bestowed the judgment Jesus predicted, and which this sign gift attested to each time it was used. It "fell away of itself."

No other purpose for tongues is given in the New Testament. It is reading beyond doctrinal teaching to make it a prayer language. As an old-time China hand said to me when I asked her what she taught about the gift of tongues (Miss Bertha Smith), "Humph! The last time I checked, the Lord understood English well enough!" To insist that it makes one feel closer to the Lord to use it is to place insulation between the believer and the Scripture, which is evidently not as profitable as it should be to meet *every* need in our life! No, says Paul, "I will pray with my understanding" also!

The obvious unanswered question, "What, then, is the

source of the tongues being used today?" My answer from Scripture is, "*This* book does not say. To say more is to go beyond the Scripture." Whatever that source may be, it also works among the Hindus and my chicken-blood-drinking voodoo priest in Haiti! "You know how, in the days when you were still pagan, you were swept off to those dumb heathen gods, *however you happened to be led.*" "When I was a child, my speech . . . [was] all childish." "Do not be childish, my friends."

Throw it against the wall, and see if it sticks!

3. The Gift of Interpretation of Tongues

Obviously, when tongues ceased, so did this gift. What was its use when it did exist? Paul helps us with this in 1 Corinthians 14:27-28. There we are told that, for the sake of the unbelieving Jew in the service, the gift of judgment may be exercised: no more than three times, and one at a time. The interpreter is needed not for the Jew, but for the uninstructed Gentile in the service (v. 23), who without someone to explain what is going on "will think you are mad." If no interpreter is present to perform the translation of this language for the Gentile, it is better not to pronounce judgment; just pray about the problem (v. 28).

From Acts 2, it can be understood that the Jew in that day frequently spoke only the dialect of his homeland. In that passage, *known* languages were used by the Spirit to pronounce judgment upon Israel (Acts 2:11). It must be remembered that Corinth was on an isthmus. It was a sailor's town, where seafaring men and travelers stopped over as their ships were being unloaded. The cargo was then transported overland a few miles to the opposite shore, to be reloaded on other ships. As a result, this congregation would be visited regularly by Jews from all over the world. The tongues were, I believe, *known* tongues. Energized by the Spirit, the judgment was given. Interpreted by the same energizing of the Spirit, it was explained to the Gentiles in the services, who otherwise would consider the members to be crazy, drunk, or both.

4. The Gifts of Healing

Once again, we must affirm that none of the "sign" gifts remain for the purpose of revealing the presence of God to the world. In the sense of *miracle*, the energizing of healing has not occurred in centuries. Now, may I hasten to add . . .

. . . *God does heal!*

This particular subject has been the source of a months-long study group by three West Memorial members who have met together without fanfare. We have searched every single Scripture in the Old and New Testament dealing with the subject! The team has consisted of an obstetrician, a psychiatrist, and an attorney who specializes in medical cases. They were most qualified to speak to this question as I worked with them. We have reported on personal visits to healers and healing clinics, and have read books on healing which range from extreme positions on both the left and the right. Although the conclusions I share in this section are my own, I pay great honor to each of those body members who have so patiently searched the Word with me.

First, notice that this is the only one of the fifteen gifts listed where the singular form "gift" is *never* used! In every single instance, the reference is made to "gifts"—*plural*—of healings (1 Cor. 12:9,28,30). Each separate healing is a gift to the body. The Scripture does not say that one person will possess a *gift* which *causes* healings to occur; only that separate acts of healings occur, as gifts.

Second, notice that the administering of this gift is not given to all in the body. "God has *appointed*" (12:28) this gift, and it will not be found in all members.

Third, notice that this gift is "set in the *called-out-ones*" (v. 28, literal Greek). The word for "called-out-ones" is sometimes translated "church," "assembly," or "congregation." It is speaking of a body of believers, precisely what Paul is describing in this entire chapter. These gifts of healing occur *within the framework of the church*, and belong to it through the body member who is healed.

Fourth, exactly who is the agent of this gift? Can it

115

spring up anywhere among the members? No, for here we have Scripture to "guide us into all truth." The gifts of healing, to be bestowed upon the body parts by the Holy Spirit, *will occur through the office of the elder*. "Is one of you ill? He should *send for the elders* of the congregation to pray over him and anoint him with oil in the name of the Lord" (Jas. 5:14). This gift belongs to *all* elders, without exception! No indication is given that *some* elders have it and some do *not*. Even as an elder has been equipped with gifts of prophecy, teaching, etc., he will also be the channel for the *gifts* of healing, to be placed upon the body parts according to the will of God. They flow through him.

How wise is our Lord! Who knows the flock any better than the undershepherd? He will know when sickness may be God's way of calling a saint home to glory. He will know when it is a judgment for unconfessed sin. He will know better than anyone else when illness has been sent to show God's grace to be sufficient, or in order that his glory might be revealed. He will know! And to him alone is given the responsibility to become a channel for the grace gifts of healing.

Fifth, what procedure is taught for the energizing of this gift? Note: the elders do not call for the sick; *the sick call for the elders!* The initiation of the request for a gift of healing comes *from* the sick one, and is an act of faith in God. It also becomes an act of spiritual submission to the undershepherds, and is in keeping with the teaching of the Word concerning this (Rom. 13:1-2).

Sixth, the use of anointing oil is directed (Jas. 5:14). The twelve, when sent out by Jesus in Mark 6:13, met many sick people whom "they anointed with oil and cured." Olive oil for centuries had been administered to those things and people who were consecrated unto the Lord. Its use in connection with the prayer of faith which follows it is a statement by the sick person and the administering elder that this is, indeed, a yielded body. It speaks of total abandonment to the Lord. It is a symbol, and *carries absolutely no saving grace* with it into the ill person. It assuredly is not a "psychosomatic medicine," intended to innerve the power of suggestion within the individual. It is an act of identification with the Head. The body member is saying, and the elder is agreeing, that here indeed is a surrendered life! That is all—but that is important.

Why are we who call ourselves Baptists so hesitant to do what the Scripture commands at this point, when we are so very careful to carry out the letter of the Word concerning water baptism? Clearly, it must be because we are afraid of being identified with the excesses and fanaticisms of commercialized faith healers. However, we simply cannot justify our position, especially when we lean too far in reaction to radicalism. Fire is not extinguished with ice, but with a backfire! Being obedient to the Word is a marvelous safeguard.

Seventh, the elders are to pray for the sick person. This is to be a "prayer of faith." Is there any other kind? When we review the first two chapters of James's letter, we understand. To him, faith without words was dead. He said, "Prove you have faith by showing me your works." The prayer of faith is one which works. It acts upon the knowledge that God is going to do what he promised he would do, and man acts accordingly. In this case, the prayer of faith is that God will, *in the future*, heal the sick one. This is revealed by the verb tense of the word "save." It uses a tense which denotes *what is going to take place*. It is the present vividly projected into the future. Further, the verb tense does not indicate for certain whether the "saving" will take place at a *point* in time, or whether it will be a *process*. It generally refers to a point in time, but it does not *necessarily* have to be one!

Eighth, the passage graphically describes the condition of the sick person. A clue to this is that he *sends for* the elder. He is bedridden. He cannot come to the elder. The Greek says, "the prayer of faith shall save [in the future] *the exhausted one*." In Hebrews 12:3 the same word is translated, "grow faint." This would indicate the state of illness in which the member of the body calls for the elder. He is not sent running to runny noses, but to those who are in deep illness.

Ninth, in the *future* (again!), the text says the *Lord* will *raise him up*. It does not say the elder will take him by the hand and raise him instantly healed out of his bed. It says the *Lord* will energize his life, in the future.

Tenth, the statement "raise him up" means "cause to rise up from a reclining posture." It indicates that in the future the exhausted one will get up out of bed. No instantaneous cure is hinted at here, nor is it indicated that the use of the prayer of faith requires that other forms of healing agents (medicines, etc.) are to be withheld.

Eleventh, we are to understand that forgiveness of sins may well be a part of this process: "And if he be one who has committed sins, it shall be forgiven him." The elder's counsel at the bedside may mean a getting right with God for the sick one. Inference is not that all sickness is punishment for sin, but that in the anointing with oil a sick person must be brought to deal with known sin. Indeed, some are sick among us, and "many sleep," because of sin (1 Cor. 11:30), and when God uses sickness to get our attention, this confession is crucial to being healed. In every case, the pattern is 1 John 1:9! Verse 16 expands this point. Confession to each other, and the following prayer requesting forgiveness, is needed for the healing of the body.

Twelfth, we conclude that the *energizing* of "one who is such as he ought to be" is powerful and effective. The healing flows as a result of the life being properly plugged in to the lordship of Christ. *That is the crux of the matter!* We may expect the "spirituals" of healing to occur within the member of the body when there is "nothing between" that life and the living Lord. The elder does not bring instant healing; he brings instant *cleansing*, from which the healing flows forth.

The illustration of Elijah's prayer life indicates that there is great power in *prevailing*, or *continuing* prayer. The elder walks by faith, trusting continually for the raising up of the consecrated, ill, body part.

What agents can we expect to be used in the raising up process? Who would disagree that, when God wants to, he can perform this without any agent except his own grace? But that does not mean he will not work through other agents. Sickness resulting from sin requires the agent of confession.

118

When illness results from breaking physical laws, and not taking proper care of the body, the agent of rest is required.

When illness results from our Lord's intention to mature the walk of the believer, the agent of time is necessary before the raising up will occur. When the illness is a part of the homegoing of a believer, the agent of healing will be death. When the illness results from an infection, the agent of healing may be an injection of penicillin. When the illness results from a broken bone, the agent may be a cast.

Beyond this careful exegesis of the Greek text, we dare not go. But we must go that far in actual practice in our body life! I share one example of this application, because it is the most outstanding one: there are dozens of less striking examples, which are just as precious in the Lord's eyes. This one, however, I shall never forget.

Within West Memorial's body for nearly five years, Betty matured from her confession and baptism into one of our truly deep members. A woman of prayer, Bible study, and discernment, she led many to Christ. As much as anyone among us, the life she lived demonstrated her great love for Christ.

In June of 1973, I was completing a Sunday evening service. My family was all packed to leave after the service for Guatemala, where I would address the missionaries during their annual meeting. During the invitation, Betty came forward. She said, "Pastor, my doctor tells me I have cataracts and require an operation. For ten days the Lord has been telling me in my prayer time that I should ask the elders to pray for me. I will be obedient to whatever you say to me. I know praying for healing has never been done in our church, but I cannot get the mind of the Lord in any other way in regard to this matter. What shall I do?"

I confess to a concern that this might breed fanaticism! I also confess that I was anxious to begin the long drive to Guatemala. I further confess that the Lord dealt with Betty's pastor during the invitation!

Without saying a word to anyone about it, Harold (the other elder), Betty, and I went to a private room at the close of the service. Both Harold and I searched our hearts and confessed all within us which would block our prayer life. Betty searched her heart likewise. Then I prayed: "Lord, I have not often been in this situation. I simply confess that I do believe that you have the power, if it is your will to use it, to bless Betty with the healing of her cataract condition. By faith, we confess together that we trust you to do what is best for her."

Following my and Harold's prayers, we simply agreed that God could affect her cataracts, and by faith we accepted that he would. During the long trip to Guatemala, Betty was often the subject of my prayer time.

Three weeks later, we returned. Betty told me she felt that her eyes were better, but there was not any way she would know for sure until the doctor examined her. A week or so later, he did so. Smiling, he reported that the usual deterioration in cases like hers had not occurred! While he could not understand it, his only suggestion was that they wait six more months before scheduling surgery. Ten months later, her eyes have continued to remain unchanged—still no deterioration!

I don't call that a "miracle." It was simply God's lovely grace-gift to a member of our body. I was the elder . . . and I attest that I had no healing power in that prayer meeting! I only know that what has happened to Betty's eyes was the work of God. There have been scores of times when I have prayed for the sick, and they have recovered by natural means. I feel no obligation to prove I'm "holy" by getting a list of healings to show off to my friends . . . I simply know, Fred, that when God wants to, he can *energize* a lovely healing as a love gift to his precious body.

Epilogue

As Fred drove down the street towards his unlit house,
the rays of the sun were just popping out of the eastern sky.
The trip had been a long one, but his body felt no need of
sleep. His heart was burning! What a difference a few simple
principles could make in the life and work of his own church
body. He listed them in his mind as he pulled into his drive-
way . . .

1. Every member of the body has gifts, and on the basis
of them, a ministry.

2. The body life can encourage the use of the basic gifts
by all; from them, more mature gifts will be manifested.

3. On the basis of recognized gifts, ministries will flow
from truly responsible members.

4. Present organizations need not be radically changed.
They need only take the shape of the actual ministers the
Head has provided for the ministry.

5. Obviously, new shapes of the church would occur as
the ministers were called by the Spirit to exercise their gifts.
But those new concepts need not be forced upon others; they
would grow out naturally.

There were other thoughts as he turned the key in the
lock of the back door of his house. How could he share these
concepts with the other members of the nominating committee? As he thought of the varied personalities represented on

it, he smiled . . . "Ver-r-r-y slow-w-w-ly." He said aloud, "Ver-r-r-y slow-w-w-ly!"

Good night, Fred. Pleasant dreams!